Beyond the Wall

Adventures of a

yellow Volkswagen *Beetle*

on the other side of

the *Iron Curtain*

MARCO CARNOVALE

Copyright © 2018 Marco Carnovale

All rights reserved.

ISBN 13: 9781790694891

To the memory of my governess Maria Persico, for me she was "ia", my second mother, who taught me much about the world until after she turned 100.

Table of Contents

PREFACE..xi

ACKNOWLEDGMENTS..xiii

INTRODUCTION..1

1. THREE STUDENTS AND A YELLOW BEETLE..............5

  11 February 1980 – Departure from Rome................................5
  12 February 1980 – Visit to Venice and Murano........................5
  13 February 1980 – From Venice to Salzburg under the Alps....6
  14 February 1980 – Salzburg..7
  15 February 1980 – On to Vienna and the Barber of Seville......8
  16 February 1980 – Drama in Vienna......................................10
  17 February 1980 – Gloom in Vienna......................................11
  18 February 1980 – New Passport in Vienna..........................11
  19 February 1980 – Uninvited to a Warsaw Pact military base 12

2. AN ACADEMIC SEMESTER IN POLAND......................21

  20 February 1980 – Finally in Poland......................................21
  21 February 1980 – Getting acquainted with Warsaw.............23
  22 February 1980 – Shopping in Warsaw................................25
  23 February 1980 – Gasoline and the Russians.......................26
  24 February 1980 – Duck and wine..28

25 February 1980 – No *amatriciana* today..................................29
27 February 1980 – Mechanics and meat-free Wednesdays.....29
28 February 1980 – Another duck...31
29 February 1980 – Socialist salaries..31
1 March 1980 – Party in the girls' student dormitory...............32
2 March 1980 – Fortune teller and full churches......................34
3 March 1980 – A plateful of bison...36
4 March 1980 – Ann is locked up in the boys' dorm................39
5 March 1980 – Palace of Culture and Science........................40
7 March 1980 – Credit, Beethoven and bear steak...................41
8 March 1980 – Concert and women's day with Polish girls...44
9 March 1980 – Churches in Warsaw.......................................45
10 March 1980 – Yet another duck, the moon and the stars.....46
11 March 1980 - Mushrooms and cream..................................47
12 March 1980 – Car wash, passport photos and cold broth....47
14 March 1980 – *Fusilli alla carbonara*..................................49
15 march 1980 – Warsaw Museum and lines for bread............49
16 March 1980 – *Łazenki*, old ghetto, change of the guard......50
17 March 1980 – Planning ahead: USSR and DDR..................52
18 March 1980 – Hope for travel to the East............................53
19 March 1980 – Pasta and music...53
20 March 1980 – Class in Polish foreign policy.......................54
21 March 1980 – Off to Lublin..54
22 March 1980 – Lublin, Tartars and Lenin..............................56
23 March 1980 – Elections for Parliament................................58
24 March 1980 – Expanding our collection of visas.................59
25 March 1980 – Jesus, *Chateaubriand* and Grignolino..........60

26 March 1980 – East German plans and Cuban coffee..........61
27 March 1980 – Socialist ideology and Cold War.................62
28 March 1980 – Socialist ping pong..64
29 March 1980 – A song for the Polish pope...........................65
30 March 1980 – News about Katyn..67
31 March 1980 – Ice skating and drinks..................................69
1 April 1980 – Train tickets to the DDR and Russian caviar....69
2 April 1980 – Shopping and more study................................71
3 April 1980 – Train tickets and church music.......................72
4 April 1980 - Bureaucracy and a concert..............................73
5 April 1980 – Częstochowa..73
6 April 1980 – Easter day procession in Jasna Gora.............75
7 April 1980 – Getting ready for East Germany.....................77
8 April 1980 – Departure to Berlin..77
9 April 1980 – A taste of East and on to the West Berlin.........78
10 April 1980 – Exploring West Berlin....................................82
11 April 1980 – *Reichstag* and *Tiergarten*.......................83
12 April 1980 – Both sides of Berlin and return to Poland........84
13 April 1980 – Walking and eating in Warsaw......................86
14 April 1980 – New Polish visa and ice cream.....................87
15 April 1980 – Meals, music and socialist toilets..................88
16 April 1980 – Mail and telephone..90
17 April 1980 – Sending letters abroad..................................91
18 April 1980 – Shopping, smoking and tea..........................92
19 April 1980 – Football and mountain climbing....................94
20 April 1980 – Stripping at a wedding..................................94
21 April 1980 – Private lodging..96

22 April 1980 – Classes and some privacy................................97
24 April 1980 – Dad and mum come to Poland........................97
25 April 1980 – A flower, a blind singer and a party................98
26 April 1980 – East-West seminar..99
27 April 1980 – Wilanow, missed Chopin and lots of food....100
28 April 1980 – Studying and cooking....................................101
29 April 1980 – Dinner, party and flags..................................102
30 April 1980 – Nourishing body and mind...........................103
1 May 1980 – International Workers' Day celebrations..........104
3 May 1980 – Telephones in the dorm....................................105
4 May 1980 – End of an era in Yugoslavia.............................106
5 May 1980 – Informal lecture on the Polish political system 107
6 May 1980 – Studying Comecon...108
8 May 1980 – Foreign Policy Exam..109
9 May 1980 – Thirty-five Years of Victory............................110
10 May 1980 – Trip to Krakow..110
11 May 1980 – Krakow visit and the Moscow Olympics.......112
12 May 1980 – Auschwitz...113
13 May 1980 – Salt mine and fine arts....................................115
14 May 1980 – Pieskowa Skala...117
15 May 1980 – Dunajec cruise and promises of liberation.....118
16 May 1980 – Zakopane and *Juwenalia*...............................119
17 May 1980 – Back to Warsaw, meet Cathy.........................120
18 May 1980 – More phone calls, customs controls, newspapers and cars..121
19 May 1980 – Soviet visa and another duck.........................123

20 May 1980 – UNESCO, engine oil and Russia's future......125
21 May 1980 – Another visa, food and dreams......127
22 May 1980 – Drive to Gniew and rock music in Gdansk....129
23 May 1980 – Gdansk money, old atlas and music......131
24 May 1980 – To Hel (one L) and back......133
25 May 1980 – Gdansk to Oliwa and the Masurian lakes......134
26 May 1980 – Rowing in the wind......136
27 May 1980 – Getting lost in the Masurian lakes region......137
28 May 1980 – Wilanow and rubles......140
29 May 1980 – Russian state exam......140
30 May 1980 – Train or plane?......141
2 June 1980 – Bureaucracy and a wedding gift......142

3. THE BEETLE DRIVES TO THE USSR......143

3 June 1980 – Off to the USSR......143
4 June 1980 – Minsk to Smolensk: Afghanistan, Bulgarian wine and the Moscow Olympics......146
5 June 1980 – Smolensk to Moscow: Red Square at night.....150
6 June 1980 – Moscow: books, champagne and army belts...154
7 June 1980 – Hard currency shopping, Kremlin museum and Bolshoi dancers......156
8 June 1980 – Highway driving and Novgorod churches......160
9 June 1980 – Novgorod to Leningrad, black market, caviar and Soviet champagne......162
10 June 1980 – Sightseeing and dining in Leningrad......165
11 June 1980 – *Petrodvorets*: moose and rocket watch......166
12 June 1980 – Churches, gasoline, romantic white nights....168
13 June 1980 – Finnish border and ferry boat to Sweden......170

4. THE BEETLE GOES HOME 172

14 June 1980 – Swedish salmon and Soviet submarines........172

15 June 1980 – Car washing and net fishing...........................173

16 June 1980 – Flags, friends and ferry..................................174

17 June 1980 – Ferry across the Baltic and back to Warsaw. .175

18 June 1980 – Crystals and corals..175

19 June 1980 – Getting ready to leave, and next steps...........176

20 June 1980 – Last day in Warsaw, for now.........................178

21 June 1980 – Drive to Przemysl..179

22 June 1980 – Hungarian police and lake Balaton................180

23 June 1980 – Through Yugoslavia and on to Italy...............181

24 June 1980 – Back to the starting line................................183

SELECTED CHRONOLOGY...185

ALPHABETICAL INDEX..189

ABOUT THE AUTHOR..193

PREFACE

I was born and grew up in Rome, Italy in a traditional family. I was very comfortable, though quite soon during adolescence I became more curious than I was comfortable. By the time I was about to finish high school I grew increasingly restless and wanted to see more of the world. The main reason for this was the example of my uncle Gigi, a professional viola player who toured the planet with his string quintet and piano quartet. He taught me to think out of the box, to look beyond the borders of my city and my country with an open mind, always ready to learn new points of view and different ways of life.

The best way to do that, for a curious teenager, was having a foreign girlfriend, which I did in a rather innocent manner when I dated (mostly via hand-written letters) a Swedish girl, but it was all too difficult in an era with no video chat. I did go and visit her a couple of times in Sweden, and she came to Italy once, but our relationship, predictably, ended very soon. However, I remained in touch with her family and they will make an appearance in the plot of this book.

The next best option was of course to attend university abroad. I decided to apply to some American colleges. I figured that America was the leader of the free world, so I might as well get to know it and maybe move there. American music, pop art, films, were irresistibly attractive to a European teenager of the mid-1970s.

Learning the English language would be an extra bonus, it would be useful even if I returned to Italy after graduation, or if I went anywhere else for that matter, whatever I would choose to do with my life.

I also wanted to live independently and move out of my parents' home. I loved them then and I miss them now. But I felt an irresistible urge to fly out of the nest, to find my way. They (especially my father) were a bit sorry I would not take over their dental practice but supported me anyway. Luckily, my younger brother Fabio, wise man he was, did, which guaranteed me continued free dental check-ups for many more years after my parents retired.

The final and decisive argument for going to America was that in those days very few European universities (none in Italy) offered courses in international relations. After a lengthy application process, tests, recommendation letters, translations of official documents, I was accepted to Georgetown University's School of Foreign Service (SFS), which I attended from the fall of

1978 to the end of 1981, where I earned a Bachelor of Science degree in international relations.

GU's SFS is a special school. It had been created after World War I to prepare America to be better engaged with the world and initially it just trained its diplomats. It later expanded to a true academic university. Many students signed up from all four corners of the world, or almost all. Virtually no one from the socialist countries of eastern Europe.

But after Deng Xiaoping's reforms a few Chinese kids, easily recognizable by their Mao-style uniforms and hats, could be seen on campus, walking together in small groups. Their expressions looked like they felt they were on Mars. I tried to befriend them, I was curious about their version of socialism. Our conversations were eye-opening experiences on the Chinese way of life.

Once one of them asked me why each of us had a "private" telephone in our dorm rooms, it was a waste of money she said. Could we not just walk to the post office if we needed to make a phone call? I thought that would be possible but then if no one had private phone lines one could only call a public office, or a business. The concept of a private phone call was alien to them.

Meeting Chinese students at college was the first sign that China would take an important place in my life. More indications of my Chinese destiny will appear in the course of this book. I would travel there a few years later, and eventually I would marry a Chinese lady, the most defining development of my whole life!

GU had a diverse and cosmopolitan faculty, with many foreign professors, and its location in Washington, DC gave the school a truly international outlook. It was the perfect milieu to learn about the world, exactly what I was looking for. The university also had many connections and joint programs with equivalent foreign institutions, and this book is about how one of these programs opened unexpected doors that I had no idea even existed.

ACKNOWLEDGMENTS

There are way too many people to thank without whom this book would not have been written. More importantly, without whom I would not have had the life-changing experiences I will try to relate in this book. First of all my parents, who did not really have a clue of what I was getting into when I told them I wanted to spend a semester in communist Poland, but did not hesitate to give me their wholehearted support to make it happen.

The two persons to whom I am forever indebted for having shared just about every hour of this trip are my travel companions Andrew and Ann. We shared many happy moments and some more somber situations together but we always supported each other and this allowed us to make the best out of our time. The three of us had very different personalities but were passionate students of the politics and the economics of Poland and the USSR. We learned a lot from each other through endless conversations and many hours studying together, comparing the reality we witnessed with our own eyes with the official version provided by our books and our Polish professors.

Andrew and I became lifelong friends and continued to exchange our views of politics and economics despite living in different continents, and we met frequently in various countries around the world.

Ann was among my closest friends at Georgetown as well, and we too met occasionally over the following years. I am grateful to her for sharing so many details from her own diary that I had missed when writing mine, and for correcting some errors in an earlier draft of this book.

It goes without saying that meeting countless Polish people was the most precious treasure the three of us found on our way. Some became friends, others remained occasional fleeting encounters, but all opened their heart to us well beyond our expectations. Because of the political and technological limitations at the time, we sadly lost touch with all the people we met while in the USSR.

Our main course tutor, Bogdan, who was in charge of coordinating all aspects of our stay, was able to walk a fine line between practical needs and official rules and his help was indispensable for us to navigate safely through the bureaucratic bottlenecks of the country. He helped with our studies, of course, but also with accommodation, tours, visas etc. He was our real Polish mentor.

Our other professors also delivered many interesting lectures, some more than others, despite their being constrained by the ideological situation at the time as to what they could say in the classroom. A lot of what we heard was simply propaganda, although, to their credit, they looked like they did not always believe themselves what they were supposed to teach us.

Many classmates made us feel at home from day one and we shared most of what constitutes this book. Stefan, Romek, Halina, Alina, Radek, Marek, Marta, Christopher, Waldek and Elżbieta are only a few among many others, those with whom we established a more special bond.

I would like to especially thank Marzena, her mother, Marian and Ewa, who went out of their way to help make our experience an unforgettable one and became very close friends even if I later lost track of them. Who knows, maybe they will read this book and get in touch. I would love to see them again.

While this book is an accurate reflection of what I honestly remember and what I wrote down in my diary at the time, in 1980, I accept sole responsibility for any errors. Some names of people mentioned have been changed.

This book is available on all Amazon websites. I can be reached at my email address: carno.polo@gmail.com.

London, December 2018

INTRODUCTION

It was common practice for students at Georgetown's SFS to sign up for a junior (third) year abroad. The school correctly imagined that no course can teach international relations better than direct experience in a foreign country. Of course, I was already "abroad" in the United States but I thought this was a unique opportunity not to be missed.

In the "Fall" academic semester of 1979 I was a "sophomore", attending my second year of college, and it was the right time to start applying for junior year abroad programs for the following academic year.

At the time I was quite shocked by what was happening in South East Asia: the Vietnam war was over but the bloodshed continued. With the Americans gone, it was largely a proxy war between the two communist superpowers: the Soviet Union and China. In Cambodia, what was probably the most bloodthirsty regime of the XX century, the Maoist *Khmer Rouge*, a friend of China, wanted to establish a rural society free of any foreign "contamination" and was decimating its own population in the process of doing so. Over a million people died. Vietnam, supported by the Soviet Union, and newly unified under communist rule, invaded Cambodia to assert its influence and prevent China from gaining a foothold in the region. As a result of this upheaval, hundreds of thousands of refugees literally ran for their life, or took to sea in rickety boats. Tens of thousands died in the process.

Thousands more however reached the relative safety of neighboring Thailand, where the Red Cross and other organizations had set up emergency camps. Georgetown offered a program whereby juniors could volunteer to work in one of these camps and get academic credit for it. I applied without hesitation. It promised to be an incredibly interesting and useful thing to do.

After a few days, much to my consternation, the Study Abroad office informed me that I had been turned down. However, they told me that, as I had shown interest in communist countries, there was space for me in another program, a student exchange that GU had agreed with the Central School of Planning and Statistics in Warsaw, Poland. Well, it was a one-way "exchange": no Polish students were allowed, or could afford, to spend a semester at Georgetown.

I was intrigued. Not as exotic as South East Asia perhaps, but I had never been on the "other side" of the geopolitical divide between capitalist and socialist countries in Europe. The catch was, I had to get ready to go pretty much right away, and start in Warsaw the following semester. I was still a sophomore, and this was meant to be a program for a junior year abroad, but they said they would bend the rule and allow me to go.

The year of 1979 was not a happy time, for East-West relations, as they were then called, ie relations between the democratic West, led by the United States, and the so-called "socialist" bloc of eastern European countries led, or one should say coaxed, by the Soviet Union. Many in Italy at the time considered the two blocs roughly equivalent in moral value, the same kind of political entity, except the two bosses were at loggerheads.

I begged to differ. No country ever wanted to leave the "West" to join the "East", while several tried to move in the other direction. East Germany in 1953, Hungary in 1956, Czechoslovakia in 1968 were the three most violent cases where the USSR had sent in tanks to repress the quest for freedom of their socialist "brothers" who wanted more western-style democracy and market economy. Poland had been close to meeting the same fate in 1976, but after multiple strikes and demonstrations things calmed down before the tanks rolled in.

Also, in 1979 the USSR was meddling in Afghanistan (it would invade in December) and the US was about to deploy new intermediate-range nuclear missiles in Europe. Besides, Mao had died in 1976 and post-Mao China and the US had concluded a stunning process of rapprochement, that had began with Nixon's visit to Beijing a few years earlier. The new Washington/Beijing entente had clear anti-Soviet overtones.

The Cold War seemed like it might turn into a hot one. All of this made the idea of going to the city where the Warsaw Pact, Moscow's response to NATO, had been signed, both more interesting and more sinister, quite intriguing and a bit scary.

The day after I received the Polish proposal from the Study Abroad office I had lunch in our college cafeteria with my best friend

Andrew, and talked to him about this opportunity. Andrew came from Pascoag, a small village in Rhode Island, the smallest of the fifty American states, and had never been abroad. He was getting top grades and being at GU, and in Washington, had quickly developed an interest for international affairs. We had gotten along very well from the start. "Would you go? I am not sure I want to spend a semester in a communist country on my own." I asked him. He thought about it for a few seconds and replied "Well I am not sure I would either, but it sounds interesting: if you go, I'll go."

The next day I went back to the Study Abroad office and told them: "Thanks for the offer of a slot in your semester program in Poland, I'll take two: a classmate is coming along." They were thrilled: not enough people had signed up for the program and it was at risk of being cancelled. In fact, before Andrew and I had signed up, the program had attracted a grand total of 2 students. One was Ann, a fellow School of Foreign Service student in her junior year. Ann was of Slovak/Polish descent and was interested in exploring not so much communism but rather the cultural background of her family. The other was Pat, who was not even studying at Georgetown but had been allowed to join the program from his college in New Jersey.

During the following days I spent some time thinking about the opportunities this semester would offer: the most attractive feature in my mind was that we would enjoy direct and relatively unfettered contact with fellow Polish students, as well as students from other socialist countries. This, I hoped, would provide priceless information and insights that would never be available through books, newspapers or television — there was, of course, no internet at that time.

It also occurred to me that to make the best of our time we would need mobility. I was not sure how reliable public transportation would be in getting around the city or the country, and I even thought we might want to tour some of the neighboring socialist countries after our course. For this reason I asked my parents to buy a car. They graciously agreed and I found a second-hand Volkswagen Beetle at a very reasonable price. I decided for a Beetle because it was a sturdy car, with a simple air-cooled 1300cc engine that any deft mechanic in the world could fix, but did not often need fixing in the first place. This one sported a canary yellow livery which earned it the nickname Giallina (the little yellow one). It had the added bonus of a manually activated sunroof that made it just irresistible.

Three months later Andrew and Ann flew down to visit me in Rome, Italy and after a few days in the eternal city the three of us were on our way to Poland. So the moment of truth had arrived, after months of preparation we were off to start our semester abroad. But to get to Poland from Italy we had to cross Austria – that part was easy, piece of (Sachertorte) cake – and Czechoslovakia with a 24-hour transit visa, very poor maps and, of course, neither GPS nor GSM, and that would turn out not to be as easy.

1. THREE STUDENTS AND A YELLOW BEETLE

11 February 1980 – Departure from Rome

Andrew, Ann and I started off from Rome at about 9:30am, a crispy Mediterranean morning with a blue sky that tempted us to open Giallina's sunroof, but it was just a bit too cold as we sped north on the autostrada del Sole, (the "Sun Highway" that runs from the north to the southernmost tip of the Italian peninsula) We reached Florence at about 2:00pm where we stopped for a short walk in the old city.

We started again after lunch and after having the car's tires checked we drove on until Mestre, a town just outside Venice. I was looking for an Agip motel I knew was in the vicinity as a convenient way to sleep and park the car avoiding expensive hotels in Venice (where cars can't go anyway) but it had closed down for good. We then booked a room at the "Vivit", a small bed and breakfast and then went to Venice to explore on foot.

Walking around this magic city was always going to be an experience to remember for life. One most memorable moment was when we approached Piazza San Marco after dinner, in fact quite late at night, at about 1:00am. It was totally, absolutely empty! An eerie sensation to see one of the most crowded places on earth completely devoid of the crowds of tourists that are usually associated with it. The ground was still shiny from the rains of the afternoon and the old fashioned street lights emanated a warm, tenuous light. We stood in silence for a long moment, taking in the atmosphere and feeling privileged, before heading back to the ferry that took us back to Mestre for the night.

12 February 1980 – Visit to Venice and Murano

Wake up at 9:00 and back to Venice by car and ferry. We went to the usual tourist spots: Rialto, San Marco with its superb Pala d'oro, the Palazzo Ducale. In the afternoon we visited Murano and its world famous glass blowers where I bought a new key-chain for Giallina, a small multifaceted crystal sphere for our trusted bright yellow VW beetle that would lead us through this trip.

Long day of walking, interrupted only by a couple of snacks and a good gelato. In the evening we ate some bread and cheese in the hotel room, accompanied by a bottle of pinot noir. We ended the day with a game of scopa, a popular card game all kids know in Italy and that is easy to learn. Hit the sack by 23:30, tomorrow was going to be a driving day to Austria.

13 February 1980 – From Venice to Salzburg under the Alps

We left Mestre at 9:45am and took the highway to Vittorio Veneto, where it ended. The highway ended here and so did World War I, with the surrender of the central powers to Italy on 4 November 1918, still observed as a national holiday in my country. It is not really "victory" which was celebrated, but the "armistice", the end of the war.

It was hard to believe that on these same rolling hills, which then become the magnificent Dolomites holiday destination, some of the bloodiest fighting of World War I took place between the Italians and a few allied divisions on the one side and the Germans and Austro-Hungarians on the other. Hemingway, member of a small contingent of Americans who also fought here after 1917, wrote some of the best pages on those dark years in his *Farewell to Arms*.

We continued on a regional road to Cortina d'Ampezzo and from there to the Austrian border. The weather was great, sunny and chilly, ideal for driving in a beautiful alpine landscape.

After refueling and changing Giallina's worn-out windshield wipers we crossed into Austria and the Grossglöckner glacier presented itself to us in all its majestic beauty, also thanks to the clear air that allowed for ideal visibility all the way to the horizon. Normally one would drive up the pass and enjoy the scenery but when we reached the start of the road winding uphill we learned that there was too much snow and the pass had been closed for several days. When we got to Austria, after rather cursory customs and passport controls the friendliness and smoothness of which we would come to miss in the coming months, we could not pass the opportunity to try a typical local sausage, a Würstel. Ann sprained an ankle on the icy ground but no big damage.

No choice but to return to Winklern, then Obervellach where we could put Giallina on a train car that took us through a tunnel to the other side of the Alps, and finally we reached Badgastein. Andrew and I alternated at the wheel, we were both relatively inexperienced drivers though I could see right away that he was usually more careful than me! And he also had a better sense of directions to find our way in totally foreign surroundings. Ann had never driven a manual shift car but manifested a desire to learn during our journey.

We got to Salzburg in the early evening and after looking around for inexpensive accommodation we settled for a room in the hotel *Wolf*, near the Mozartplatz. Right, Mozart, the enduring champion of Salzburg.

Of Salzburg, yes, but not of Austria. A German friend of mine pointed out to me how the Austrians pulled this incredible trick in persuading the world that Hitler was German and Mozart was Austrian. In fact, Hitler was of course an Austrian who then became a naturalized German. Mozart, however, was never Austrian. During his sadly short lifetime (1756-1791) Salzburg was the capital of the eponymous Archbishopric, which was part of the Holy Roman Empire, Germany's predecessor state if you will.

Salzburg only became part of the Austrian Empire after the Congress of Vienna in 1815, almost a quarter of a century after Mozart's death! That Wolfgang Amadeus worked in Vienna for much of his life did not make him an Austrian any more than his Italian rival Salieri or so many other foreign musicians who moved to what was then the world's music capital.

Here you could find Mozart chocolates and cards, Mozart liqueurs, Mozart pictures and pillows, magnets and mugs, the man was bringing in money to his hometown two hundred years after passing away, and not just with his music!

Quiet evening in town, a short walk, a casual dinner and then to bed. It was rather cold and it felt colder because it was damp.

14 February 1980 – Salzburg

Breakfast at 9:00am, followed by a quiet walk downtown. We visited first the cathedral, where Mozart was baptized, then the Franziskanerkirche, a sober yet intense moment.

After that we climbed up to the Hohensalzburg (high Salzburg, predictably situated on top of a hill) fortress. It was a cloudy day and a pretty cold one in Salzburg, the city of salt, from the barges laden with the precious cooking ingredient that passed through the city in antiquity on the aptly named river Salzach.

In the afternoon we visited Mozart's family home, where he was born and grew up studying music non-stop under the watchful eye of the father. I wondered whether he was a happy child. I guess probably not, but he would make millions happy for centuries to come. Later in the afternoon a sweet stop at the *Fuerst Konditorei*, a pastry shop on the Brodgasse, for a big chunk of chocolate *torte*!

Slow walk in town in the evening, nothing much, just a peaceful walk in an atmosphere charged with history where Mozart's notes somehow kept ringing in my mind. Andrew was not feeling too well and called it a day early, while I had a *Wienerschnitzel* (thin veal steak covered with a crust of bread crumbs in egg batter) with Ann in a small restaurant near our hotel.

15 February 1980 – On to Vienna and the Barber of Seville

We left Salzburg at 10:00 in the morning for an easy and pleasant drive through the Austrian hillside all the way to Vienna. We were now at the edge of what we referred to as "western Europe", though neutral Austria was neither a member of NATO (the political-military alliance led by the United States) nor of the European Economic Community (the attempt by some western European countries to pool together resources and open their markets so as to break the vicious circle of wars of the last few centuries). But it was, so to speak, on our side of the great European divide referred to as the "iron curtain". It was Churchill who coined the term after World War II, to indicate the partition between free western Europe and Soviet-dominated "eastern Europe".

If you looked at the map though, Prague lied to the west of Vienna, and Czechoslovak, Polish and Hungarian history had at least as much, or more, ties to France, Germany and Italy than to Russia. So what was *East* and what was *West* lied really in the eyes of the beholder, or more precisely the eyes of Stalin, Churchill and

Roosevelt, who partitioned Europe at the Yalta conference toward the end of World War II.[1]

Austria was capitalist, and a healthy multi-party democracy governed by the rule of law. On the other side of the Danube we could see Bratislava, Czechoslovakia, a socialist country governed by a single (Communist) party and under strict control from Moscow.

In Vienna, we were at the edge, ready, excited but also a little concerned about the next step: raising the curtain and driving through, then explore for a few months. Just the three of us, with difficult means of communication with either our homes or our university, not much money and as a sole point of contact a Polish professor whose name, Bogdan, had been provided to us before we left Georgetown.

In the evening we got tickets to watch *The Barber of Seville* by Gioacchino Rossini at the *Wiener Staatsoper*, the world famous Vienna State Opera house. Great show! We were ecstatic. The *Barbiere* is incredibly powerful yet playful music: that was the genius of Rossini.

Afterwards we found a restaurant called *Paulusstube* (Paul's Pub) to eat another typical *Wienerschnitzel*. A funny situation arose when we asked whether it came with a choice of side dish, as in America a piece of meat would usually be served with some potatoes or vegetables. "It comes with nothing" was the peremptory answer of our otherwise friendly, tall and very round waiter. The problem was we had very little Austrian schillings on us as we had used most of it for our opera tickets, and so the choice was between a side order or a drink. Our tasty *Schnitzel* with nothing was therefore, of course, profusely irrigated with cold Austrian beer, after which we hit the sack very happy of our day.

---

1 *Yalta is a town in Crimea, a peninsula on the Black Sea, that was part Soviet Russia during the war, then "donated" by Khrushchev to Soviet Ukraine in the 1950s, then part of independent Ukraine and forcibly annexed by independent Russia in 2014. Here the three leaders met in February 1945, as the war in Europe was close to its end, and decided on the spheres of influence each of their countries would command in Europe after the defeat of the Axis.*

16 February 1980 – Drama in Vienna

A day that started well with a tour of the imperial *Schoenbrunn* (beautiful fountain) imperial palace turned into one of the worst nightmares of my life. I had been to the palace before, and every time it was more impressive in its elegant grand style. But what I remembered the longest was the small bedroom of the emperor Franz Joseph II. Frugal furniture and small single bed.

After the tour, we went to the large and crowded *Westbanhof* (western railway station), for a quick and cheap lunch. Which we got, no problem. We ate standing up at some tall tables. I was carrying all my essentials (passport, wallet, etc.) in a small shoulder bag, which I took off to eat and put on a shelf just under my table. Where I left it after we were done eating and we all walked back to the car for further exploration of the city.

I only realized my blunder a few minutes later. By then we had left the station and were driving in town, I turned around and sped back as fast as possible, but the bag was gone. I made a feeble attempt to ask the lady at the counter whether she had seen it or perhaps someone had turned it in. She began to shake her head before I was even finished talking. It was a busy railway station cafeteria and she, quite understandably, had not seen anyone take it away.

This was going to be a problem, not so much for the money as for my passport and even more so for my Czechoslovak transit visa and Polish student visa, without which it would be impossible to continue my journey. The iron curtain would not be raised for me after all. Were months of preparation going to be in vain? I felt so dumb and, for a brief moment, powerless.

Yet I never lost hope. I knew this could be made right and started calling home to see if mum and dad could help me get a new passport at the Italian Embassy in Vienna. A procedure which could take weeks, but my country being Italy, where organization might be wanting but common sense sometimes prevails over procedures, I was hoping a couple of phone calls might allow all of us to continue on our journey with minimal delay.

17 February 1980 – Gloom in Vienna

A gloomy Sunday. The sky was gray just like my mood. Most everything was closed down, not much to do except trying to cheer myself up for the loss of my passport. I began contemplating a precipitous flight back to Rome to sort things out.

I could easily get a piece of paper from the embassy, a *foglio di via*, a kind of warrant, to allow me to go home, but not to travel anywhere else. We considered that perhaps, in light of the uncertainty, the best thing to do would be for Andrew and Ann to drive on with Giallina, and I would join them in Warsaw later.

Ann and Andrew were good comfort in a difficult moment. Ann and Andrew were good comfort in a difficult moment. Just to be ready tomorrow and not waste any time, we went to a police station to report the theft of my bag. I was even able to draw a smile across my face while trying to put together a few words in German with the policeman at the typewriter.

A couple of *Sachertorte* (world famous Viennese chocolate cake) and an opulent dinner of wild game and red wine helped too. We hit the sack early, tomorrow I would have to rise early and try and get a new passport!

18 February 1980 – New Passport in Vienna

I was in front of the gate of the Italian consulate at 8:30, before it had opened its doors for the week. Then, an endless series of phone calls began, but in the end it all worked out for the best. I had a new passport by the end of the morning and a new Polish visa (albeit a temporary one, I would need to apply for another one when I got to Warsaw) in the afternoon! The Polish clerk was actually sympathetic: he said because we did not have enough proof of our university program with us all he could do was to get me into the country, and I would have to sort it out later.

The Czechoslovak consulate provided me with a transit visa as well, though they were a bit more on the grumpy side compared to their Polish colleagues.

In the evening we had dinner in our hotel room with a bottle of Italian merlot to wash down some dark bread, salami and cheese. We were relieved and happy to be able to continue our adventure together and celebrated the new passport while getting psychologically ready to cross the "curtain" tomorrow.

We knew we had a memorable day ahead of us, but we did not yet know how memorable!

19 February 1980 – Uninvited to a Warsaw Pact military base

We left Vienna fairly early in the morning and crossed into Czechoslovakia armed with our transit visas. Our goal was to reach Poland by the end of the day. The Austrians waved us through, while the Czechoslovaks greeted us with machine guns and barbed wire. Nevertheless we cleared customs quickly, a little more than ten minutes. The border was clearly marked by kilometers of sinister barbed wire (literally an "iron curtain") as far as the eye could see, and there was a wide no-man's land on either side of it.

We could see very few cars on the Czechoslovak side, while many buses and trucks slowed us down quite a bit. Almost all cars were either FIAT 124 (Soviet made Lada) or Czechoslovak Skoda. The road to Brno and beyond was dotted with hundreds of small monuments to communism and red banners hailing to socialism. Many large and solemn monuments were dedicated to Soviet military hardware from World War II.

One such banners read: "Our union with Russia is a guarantee of peace". I wondered how many locals really agreed with that statement, only twelve years after Russia's tanks crushed their desire for more freedom. Surely not many. But in a way the signpost was right: if Czechoslovakia had broken free of the USSR in 1968, there could have been an escalation of nationalist and democratic movements across eastern Europe. The relatively stable division of the continent agreed to at the end of World War II would have been shaken to its foundations with unpredictable consequences.

Big and small red stars, often together with hammers and sickles, were ubiquitous, on lamp posts, street signs, gates, everywhere. It was a tad intimidating, but we knew we would not stay long in the country. We had a transit visa through Czechoslovakia which allotted us only 24 hours to pass through the country, and all we possessed to find our way was a very large scale map by the American Automobile Association which had all of eastern Europe on it, few details and was probably very out of date. Yet,

Czechoslovakia had a long but narrow shape, like a banana if you will, so once we left Austria to the south we only had to drive a couple of hundred kilometers or so before we would bump into Poland on its northern side. Very easy, in theory, we thought we would need much less than one full day.

Driving along the highway that was delineated on the map, we suddenly reached its end somewhere around the town of Olomouc. The highway did not end on the map, on paper, but in reality it did, in a pile of mud! We were facing banks of mud. Ann was sitting in the back of the car, threw back her head and laughed, the situation was so ludicrous. We took another turn and got a beautiful late afternoon view of a mountainous area.

At one point we reached a fork and there was a large sign in Czech that explained the detour we were supposed to take, so we sat there for a little while trying to decipher it. After a while, we thought we had a rough idea of which way to go, so we moved on, but it soon became clear we were going nowhere. We tried to communicate with some old Czech ladies we met by the roadside but that didn't help much, though they were very kind and did allow Ann to use a toilet which relieved her considerably.

So we drove back to the fork with the large sign in Czech and decided to try our last option, a very nice road with no traffic, smooth asphalt, and a really beautiful landscape. It did not seem to go north, the way we wanted to go, but we had no other choice left and in any case, we thought, wherever we would end up we could not be far from Poland.

One consideration should have alerted us: we were the only travelers on the road. We stopped to ask directions and were told to go back to Olomouc. We retraced our steps to the sign at the fork and studied it for a few moments. The Czech text remained largely a mystery, but it seemed that the sign depicted the detour. We became increasingly unsure when we saw signs with "WOJ" blazoned across, which Ann worryingly translated as "ARMY".

We were winding our way through the mountains of Czechoslovakia and the sun was slowly setting, so it was now early evening. We were still confident we had to be going in the right direction because it was the only road. After a little while we came to a small signpost with no words, just a black silhouette of a tank on a yellow background.

We looked at it, and at each other, and thought: "So what?" It was the only road, we had no choice, we should just drive on. At this point Ann, who had stopped laughing and had become very serious, implored us to turn around, even if that meant we would have to go back to Vienna and try again tomorrow, or whenever we would manage to get new visas. But that would have forced us to try to find our way to Austria in the dark, with no useful map and no chance to ask anyone for directions. We would likely end up lost either way. Andrew and I voted to keep going.

After a short while we came across a few houses. It was a quaint village, kind of neat and tidy. Some soldiers were walking around, so we stopped one of them and tried to ask him for directions to get back to the highway towards Poland. Ann told him in Russian that we were lost. He seemed a bit surprised and was not especially helpful. All he knew how to say was: "Passport, passport."

We did not know why he wanted our passports, but we were in no position to argue, so we handed them over and saw him walking away. This is when we began to feel a bit of uneasiness. He went into this little phone booth by the roadside and made a couple of phone calls. Meanwhile, we got out of the car and were trying to talk to him. Between the three of us, we spoke enough of six different European languages to carry on a decent conversation in English, French, German, Italian, Russian and Polish, though sadly not much Czech except for Ann who knew a few words.

He did not understand any of them, however, or so he pretended, so we could not communicate. He called someone else who spoke German, who ordered us to follow them with the car to where they were walking. "Langsam" (German for "slowly"), he added. We did, and found ourselves in this little compound. By now it was about 6:00 p.m. There was ice all over the place, and it was pretty cold. He just told us to wait out there for him. So we were out there waiting for about 45 minutes, and by then it was completely dark and freezing cold.

There were soldiers arriving at the building and entering, including a few officers (we could tell officers by the stripes on their hats and their epaulets, which made us think something important was coming up). It looked like they were trying to figure out what to do. I supposed they had trained for all kinds of military threats but not for an invasion by a yellow Volkswagen beetle loaded with college students.

After a while they came out and they called me in. So we started to realize that something must be quite wrong. By this time we knew we were on a Warsaw Pact army base because there were soldiers everywhere. We tried to go in together but they said: "No, Marco! No, Marco!" They were already on a first name basis with me!

They took me into this room in which there were a couple of officers with red bands around their hats as well as a few soldiers. One of them was an interpreter – he spoke German. He was the only one I could speak with because not one of them spoke English, let alone Italian. I had just had a year and a half of training in German at GU, so I was far from fluent, but it was enough for the purpose of being interrogated by adversarial Communist officers.

On the wall of the room they had large medallions with pictures of Lenin and a poster of him, as well as a picture of Felix Dzerzhinsky, the founder of the Cheka, the Soviet Secret Police, as the KGB was then called: I knew Lenin but did not immediately recognize Dzerzhinsky's face and asked who he was.

Someone replied he was the founder of the Soviet secret police. I replied: "Do you mean of the Czechoslovak secret police?". Answer: "No, no, the Soviet secret police". Of course, silly me.

Also on the wall, rather more predictably, was a picture of the president of Czechoslovakia. And there was a guy sitting at a typewriter to record the session. They interrogated me for an hour and a half in German. That was the first time I used my German other than in classroom and I must say that if I had been less scared I would have been rather proud of myself.

My interrogator started out: "Did you see the yellow sign of the tank on the road?"

I said: "Yes I did."

Interrogator: "Did you realize that you should not drive on through because there was a no trespassing sign?" he continued.

I replied: "Yes, I did, but we had no choice because we tried all the other roads, and we could not get anywhere. We have to get to Poland within six hours as our transit visa through Czechoslovakia is about to expire."

He said: "What if you had found such a sign in a military base in your country? What would you have done?"

I said: "I would have turned back because I would have known where to go."

Six times I had to show them on the map our itinerary through Czechoslovakia – which cities we had been going through, or rather where I thought we had been.

And they kept asking me: "Who are you, Marco? What are you carrying? You are studying in America – why are you studying in America? Do you know of military bases in Italy?"

By this time I was half scared and half amused: "I am studying international relations in the United States because that is where I found a program I liked, but I do not know any Italian base. I have not been in the army yet."

Interrogator: "Do you know about military bases in the United States?"

I responded: "Well, not much but I know there is an air force base near Washington; it's called Andrews Air Force Base. Maybe that would interest you."

So he wrote that down. And he kept asking me why I had trespassed the line if I knew I should not get through. And I kept replying I did but I also knew we did not have any other choice; we had to go to Poland, and we only had six hours left to get the hell out of there. (I did not really know how to say "the hell out of" in German but that's what I thought as I spoke.) Before I could get up from my chair to rejoin my friends they gave me a multiple-page document to sign. I had not idea what it said as it was in Czech. Actually I did have an idea, it was probably some sort of confession of my trespassing crime and who knows what else about military bases in NATO countries.

Meanwhile, the others were literally freezing outside the building. Andrew and Ann were sitting there debating what they ought to do, when Andrew remembered we had a frisbee and a football in the trunk. So he took them out of the car and about this time I emerged from my interrogation and joined them. So we tried playing frisbee to kill time and, more importantly, keep warm, but we could not really grip it because it was too cold.

At this point they called Ann into the interrogation room because they had at long last found someone who spoke Russian, which was Ann's second language. That it took them so long was surprising because all Czechoslovak officers were supposed to learn

Russian. In fact, pretty much everyone in the country had to study it in school.

As Ann walked into the interrogation room she saw the same paintings of communist notables on the wall I had seen but wisely did not ask any questions. In a corner at her left stood a Czech officer, with red stripes and a few stars on his shoulders. To her left was a Czech at a typewriter, her interrogator.

For one hour and a half or so they interrogated her directly in Russian about everything imaginable. First they wanted to know (again) our exact routes, which towns we passed through and where we got lost. She told them we lost route 46 somewhere near the town of Šternberk, which was more precise and therefore different from what I had said. "Aaaah!" he tried to corner her, "your friend said you got lost somewhere else". She did not know what I had said, and could not be sure of where exactly we had gotten lost so she faltered and was prompted to say we lost E7 at Olomouc.

As she faltered some more, both to remember details and also to express herself in Russian, he charged that she was a spy. It took a moment for the Russian word "*shpion*" to register and, when it did, it sounded so ludicrous she said, in English, "Oh boy, come on!"

They asked if she had ever been in Czechoslovakia before and wanted to know the exact towns and whom she visited. She had to hum and haw over that one as in fact she had been in the country in 1974 with her parents to visit relatives in Slovakia - her mother's uncle and first cousins. Of course, the last thing Ann wanted was to get those people in trouble by revealing their association with a spy, so she omitted that bit of information.

They asked about the courses she was taking in college, why she wanted to go to Poland, if she knew any Czech immigrants to the United States. She hum and hawed over that one too. And finally they wanted to know about American military bases, about which she knew nothing.

In the end they made her sign a two-page document written in Czech and told her she had to pay a fine of 100 Czechoslovak koruna, about 4 dollars. She handled all of this by herself, as her "interpreter", who did not do any interpreting anyway, had come outside to play football with Andrew and me.

When Ann came back outside to the dark freezing evening, my German interpreter, who turned out to be a law student and really nice guy named Paul, came out and joined us. Another guy, one of the guards, came over and picked up the football. Paul thought it was rugby. We told him it was a brand new American football Andrew had bought to play with our future Polish classmates, and another guard exclaimed, "Oh, Joe Namath!" I had no clue who Joe Namath was, and on this occasion I learned he was a star American football player of the sixties and early seventies.

We showed them all how to throw the football. I was not that good but Andrew had some experience in spinning the ball into a long parabolic trajectory. Then a couple of other guards joined in. The big guard knew he was supposed to tackle the others. He did not know exactly how, so Andrew showed him how to assume a football stance and set the other guy up in one as well. Then he showed them that I would pretend to hike. I indicated they were supposed to hit each other. They said, "Okay." And proceeded to do it!

All of a sudden there was a group of twenty or thirty very drunk soldiers coming down the hill. I could not understand what they were saying, but it seemed very coarse. I asked about them, and one soldier said: "Oh, don't worry about them; they are just Russians. They are always this way." So we started asking about the Russians at the base but unsurprisingly they refused to answer any question even remotely related to the military.

I wanted to take a picture of us playing, or of the Russians, but they responded that it would not be a good idea. One officer curtly specified that they would take the camera away and jail us.

As we were playing football, the guy who had interrogated me picked up some hot drinks for us and went to his room. He returned a few minutes later with a little Statue of Liberty (about ten centimeters tall) which he showed us with some circumspection as clearly he did not want any superior officer to see that. He said his uncle had taken it from New York in 1931, or some time around then. He had kept that little statue and was always carrying it with him, even on a Warsaw Pact base!

Paul, my German interpreter, was genuinely interested in keeping in touch with me and took my address although he said he would not be allowed to write to me. Of course, there was no question of me writing to him while he was in the army.

The guy who interrogated me was a lot nicer when he was away from the officers. He asked if we were hungry. We replied that yes we were in fact. By now it was 9 p.m. and we had not eaten or drunk anything since the morning and were very hungry. The interpreter wanted to take us to this military cafeteria, but the officers would not allow him. They said, matter-of-factly, that it was not allowed to take foreigners to a military restaurant. I imagined they feared we could steal some secret military recipes and transmit them to NATO.

Finally the guys with whom we were playing football were instructed to escort us to the border, so that felt really good, they were nice guys. The other officers got a jeep and said: "You get back in your car and follow the jeep. Do not try and go anywhere else, just follow the jeep." Which of course we were more than happy to do.

When we got to the border, our custodian angels got out of their cars to shake our hands and take us to the customs official and through passport control. We walked into a dimly lit booth and handed in our passports. Nothing to declare, we are going to Poland to study for a few months.

We presented our papers, and the border guard, who was obviously bored by a very quiet night with no traffic at the border station, said in broken English: "Ooooh, I can see you have been assessed a fine."

We said: "Yeah that's right, we have indeed." By this time we ready to pay whatever they asked and just wanted to get it over with as fast as possible and move on to Poland.

The soldiers escorting us said something to explain what had happened but the border guard just chuckled and threw our papers into a drawer, and we did not pay anything. They added: "Now you have to leave the country."

Andrew replied with anticipation: "Fine, show us the way!"

They escorted us for the few meters remaining to the border and we were off the hook. The Polish guards on the other side of the border were grey faced, or perhaps just tired as it was getting very late, and let us in without as much as a comment.

We crossed into Poland just after midnight and it was early on 20 February when we reached the town of Cieszyn, checked into the first nondescript hotel by the name of *Pod Selenia* ("Under Selenia" I think, though I could not for the life of me imagine who Selenia could be that someone would want to be under her) we found on our way. It was pitch dark and very cold.

It had been a pretty intense day and we were exhausted but also elated for the extraordinary adventure we had just lived through. What happened on this day was one of the defining days of my life, no less. It was not funny when it happened, though already that very night, as I collapsed exhausted in my bed, I was sure it would make for countless hilarious conversations for years to come.

2. AN ACADEMIC SEMESTER IN POLAND

20 February 1980 – Finally in Poland

I woke up early in the morning, feeling a bit exhausted by the unforeseen events of the last few days but relieved to be in Poland, all three of us together, with passports, visa and Giallina in good shape, and headed onward to Warsaw. Sadly, we never met Selenia.

First we needed money however, and as it had been impossible to buy Polish currency outside of Poland we now had to exchange some US dollars at the official rate (1 USD = 29 złoty). We were aware that the official rate was a rip-off, as it was kept artificially high, well above its real market value. But, for today, we had no choice. We walked into the first bank we saw, and proceeded to change a couple of hundred dollars for our first expenses.

The second thing we needed, even more urgently than money, was fuel to fill up Giallina's tank. This time we would have loved to buy gas at the official price (very cheap) but foreigners were not allowed to and had to buy special gas *coupons* at a much more expensive price per liter, which could then be exchanged for fuel at any gas station. In Italy at the time we also had *coupons* for foreigners, but this allowed them to buy gas at a *cheaper*, mostly untaxed, price. Here foreigners were supposed to pay more than locals.

We thought this was rather unfair and wondered whether there might be a way around it, since the gas stations did not seem to keep a record of whom they actually sold the fuel to, local or foreigner.

We reached Warsaw in the late afternoon. As we approached downtown I parked by the sidewalk of a large boulevard and walked to a public phone booth by the roadside and called Bogdan, our professor/supervisor at the Central School of Planning and Statistics whose name and number had been provided to us at Georgetown. He was in charge of the exchange program with Georgetown University.

He was surprised to hear from us this late in the day, of course he had no idea we had been driving all the way from Italy, he thought we would fly to Poland like any normal people and arrive for the official start of the academic semester in March.

Obviously there had been some miscommunication with the Study Abroad office at Georgetown. He was having dinner at home, I think he even had guests over, but he very kindly directed us to have a cup of coffee at the *Forum* hotel where he would came to meet us and lead us to our dorms.

As we waited we made bets on what he would look like: he turned out to be a pleasant and in Ann's view even "cute" young man of about thirty-five years, about 1.75cm and speaking pretty good English with a slight British accent. Ann won on most counts.

Andrew and I were assigned to the male dorm, at n. 22 on Madalinski street. He was a hero of the failed Polish uprising against the Prussians in 1794, after which the country was carved up between Russia, Prussia and Austria and ceased to exist for over 120 years. The dorm was named after the Greek god Hermes (Mercury for the Romans).

Our room (n.325) was rather large if not so well appointed. We dropped our bags and went on with Ann and Bogdan to the female dorm, just a few hundred meters away. As the female students' house was a bit overcrowded, Ann would share a room with three other girls: Alina, Halina (aka Bonga) and Elżbieta.

They lived in what was appropriately called the *Sabinki* dormitory. The Sabines were ladies who, according to an ancient legend, where kidnapped by the all-male followers of the first Roman king Romulus, who needed lots of wives to have enough children to build up the new nation. The name sounded to me like this place might be a fair hunting ground for Andrew and me for the next few months!

We thanked Bogdan who left us to go back to his guests and spent the rest of the evening (and early morning, until about 3am) with the girls, getting acquainted and sipping the first of what over the next few months would become an extraordinarily long series of shots of Polish vodka.

This time it was *Wyborowa*, a popular brand in the country, which means "choice", though we did not have any choice but to keep toasting with our new friends! Pretty bottle, designed by the famous architect Frank Gehry as I was told. I did not know architects designed bottles in addition to buildings, but I suppose a bottle is just another kind of structure intended to improve our quality of life.

The girls turned out to be extraordinarily welcoming, they offered us lots of food, and were obviously ecstatic to have unexpected foreign (and western!) colleagues in their midst. It was not the first time it happened, but it was a rare occurrence, the East-West divide made academic exchanges more unnecessarily complicated than they would have been otherwise.

21 February 1980 – Getting acquainted with Warsaw

Morning with Bogdan, who took us around SGPiS and explained how everything worked, or didn't. He then took us for a walk in the Marszałkowska, one of the main avenues of the city. First impression was of a general sadness. No one smiled in the streets. Everything looked a bit shabby. The predominant color was grey: people, buildings, road, sidewalks, mud, slush, cars, sky, all grey.

I noticed how cars here were parked *on* the sidewalks and not just next to them as in the rest of the world I knew. Also, their owners had removed their windshield wipers for the night. Or for the day for that matter, just anytime they left the car alone. Bogdan explained that wipers were a rare commodity, and got stolen easily. So did light bulbs for cars' lights, but not as much. And it was more complicated to take them out every day so light bulbs were mostly left in place. I knew there was a chronic problem of spare parts for cars in Poland but would never have guessed it was that bad!

In the evening we paid a visit to Ewa and Marian, two friends of Italian friends. They made ends meet by doing a bit of everything, including selling telephone parts to Italian handset manufacturers. They lived in a nondescript apartment building in the outskirts of the city but were doing pretty well by local standards. We had a great evening with them and two Swedish lady friends of theirs who were there.

Of course we were treated to a Gargantuan dinner, the first of an endless series of such libations in Poland, during which we received the first of many lessons on the "real economy" in Poland. In a nutshell, whereas Bogdan gave us a more official explanation of how things were supposed to work, understandably given his official capacity, our hosts told us how things in reality did not work. And, more importantly, how you could make things work, virtually all the time, with unofficial and unorthodox methods. All of this we heard partly in Italian, partly in Polish and a little bit in English.

We stayed there until 3am (this seemed like it was going to become a habit) and exchanged our first "black" money, 110 złoty for a dollar instead of the official rate of 29-to-1, quite a good deal for us. With these dollars, our Polish friends could by stuff that was only available in special hard-currency-only stores, called *Pewex*. The name *Pewex* came from the unpronounceable (for me) **P**rzedsiębiorstwo **E**ksportu **W**ewnętrznego, ie Internal Export Company. (Not sure where the final X came from.)

Pewex was, in a nutshell, the symbol of the socialist economy's utter failure in the country. It worked like this: because the socialist planned system was inefficient, it could not provide many goods for people to buy, and especially it could not afford to supply imported stuff. So the Communist party decreed: we will allow a government-owned company, *Pewex*, to import these goods and sell them in Poland, but for dollars (or Deutsche Marks, perhaps British Pounds or Swiss Francs). So, strictly speaking, the good were being re-exported to dollar-holding buyers. But since these lucky individuals were in Poland, it was an internal export, as opposed to a normal, external export that occurs when something is sold to a buyer who is in another country. Rather convoluted verbal gymnastics, yet it was useful to understand the system. But the plot thickened.

In theory Poles were not allowed to own dollars in cash, they had to deposit them into dollar accounts of state controlled banks. Most Poles however did own dollars and spent them at *Pewex*. But because these dollars were often acquired through illegal activities, they did not want to deposit in a bank account where they would be visible to the authorities. However we foreigners could hold dollar cash and spend it at *Pewex*. So they often asked a foreign friend to go in and buy on their behalf.

In this way everyone was happy: the people got the goods, the government made a profit in dollars, and even foreign visitors like us could have easy access to otherwise nowhere-to-be-found items, from electronics to good toothpaste.[2]

---

2 *After the 1989 collapse of the system, with the Polish currency freely exchangeable and trade more open to world supplies, Pewex lost its raison d'être. It was first privatized and then went bankrupt in the mid-1990s.*

22 February 1980 – Shopping in Warsaw

We spent the morning with Bogdan setting up the course schedule and sorting out many small issues related to our stay here over the next several months. He was a quiet person who acted calmly and deliberately. He was obviously elated to be managing this exchange program with a well known American university.

He insisted, correctly, that we take Polish language classes every day. We learned basic Polish very quickly (Ann was actually already fairly fluent) and that opened many doors over the following months, both figuratively and literally.

Speaking of Polish language. When Ann visited our dorm so we could all go out and visit the city, she learned that the system was that she had to give her I.D. card at the desk. When she did, she had to say the number of the room (ours, 325) she was going to visit. In Polish 325 is "trzysta dwadziescia pięć". She did such no problem.

Impressed with herself, once she reached our room she commented to us: "You know, three months ago, I would have died before I would have been able to say 'trzysta dwadziescia pięć'".

To which I honestly remarked "I probably will die before I can say 'trzysta dwadziescia pięć'"!

In the afternoon the three of us explored the city. First we went to *Supersam*: the modernist structure of the first self-serve supermarket to open in Poland housed an array of aisles with shelves stacked (or not) with quite unappealing groceries. I noticed especially long lines at the meat counter. There was some meat there to be had, but not much choice and its appearance was rather, well, unappealing. Poles loved their meat, as we would soon learn, whenever they could get their hands on some. As we walked in one of the staff insisted that each of us take a shopping basket, maybe to keep count of how many people get in, I was not sure. When we left we just put the empty shopping baskets in a pile by the exit door.[3]

We then went into a shop to buy a floor lamp. Andrew and I noticed our room 325 in the *Hermes* dorm was rather dark, especially in the long Polish winter, and could use some additional illumination. We considered that we could not possibly take the lamp with us at the end of the term but the expense was minimal and we would find

---

3   *Supersam, the modernist supermarket of Warsaw, did not survive the post-communist transition and was finally demolished in 2006.*

someone to give it to, or maybe we would just leave it in room 325 for the following occupants to enjoy.

Our final socialist shopping experience for the day was a large clothing department store called *Moda Polska*. I knew little about fashion and cared even less, but this looked really cheap and not cheerful stuff. It was run, of course, by a state-owned company and had been open for business since 1958, trying to provide some elements of fun and fashion to the otherwise drab socialist attires available elsewhere. With limited success in my humble opinion.[4]

Later I went with Bogdan to the local police office to renew the temporary visa I had been given at the Polish consulate in Vienna, I now needed a full-fledged student visa to justify my relatively long permanence in the country and also to get discounted rates at hotels all over Poland. Easily done, no problems.

By the end of the afternoon the three of us went out again exploring assorted stores where we found that prices were quite low for most Poles, and ridiculously so for us. The shelves were pretty well stacked up with merchandise but again the quality was so low. The same could be said of the cars we saw in the streets: many of them, there was even the occasional traffic jam, but mostly cheap locally made FIAT 126s and Soviet *Ladas* (also FIATs, but the bigger 124 model).

23 February 1980 – Gasoline and the Russians

The three of us had breakfast (for 13 US cents!) at the *Bar Mleczny* (literally a "milk bar" but really a sort of cafeteria) after which Marian came to meet us and took us to a gas station in town where he knew the owner and made an introduction so we could now buy gasoline at the "Polish" price, without *coupons*, and pay in złoty. Fuel has two prices in Poland, one (low) for locals and one (high) for foreigners. He charged us 25 złoty per liter instead of the official price of 16 złoty, so he pocketed 9 złoty per liter but this was still a huge saving for us. *Coupons* cost 60 black market US cents per liter, ie about 55 złoty.

---

4 *Moda Polska also did not survive the influx of foreign competition after the communist system collapsed in 1989. It tried to adapt by improving the quality of its offer but finally went under in 1998.*

I wondered how the government could provide cheap gasoline as Poland did not have any oil and suffered from a chronic deficit in its international trade balance? The answer: politics. Energy in Poland was cheap because it was provided at subsidized rates by the USSR. It was a price Moscow was willing to pay to contain discontent in the satellite countries and avoid a repetition of the dramatic and embarrassing experiences of Hungary in 1956 and Czechoslovakia in 1968.

We celebrated our full tank with a great lunch at the restaurant of the hotel *Victoria*. As we parked Giallina in front of the hotel some guy asked us whether we wanted the car cleaned: 1.50 USD for the job. OK deal. We asked that he only cleaned the outside of the car, we did not really want to leave him access to the inside. The last thing we needed was for some car cleaner to drive away with our car at the beginning of our stay. I thought of removing the wipers but decided to trust the man after all and we just walked inside.

The restaurant was called *Canaletto* and two large paintings of the Venetian master were hanging on its walls to be admired by the patrons. The paintings depicted in exquisite detail two scenes of Venice, St. Mark square and the grand canal. Our food was good and great value and after one last look at the Canaletto paintings we came out to find Giallina looking really refreshed and squeaky clean.

After lunch we went for a walk and some coffee in the *Stare Miasto* (the old city). The charming downtown had been reconstructed after having been completely destroyed by the Nazis during WW II. It was an exact replica of the original that was lost forever.

A student named Ryszard invited Ann down to translate for him some Pink Floyd songs. More likely he wanted to make a move on her, so the three of us went down together to visit and met his roommate Chris and two girls, Ewa and Anna. Halina dropped by too. I am not sure Ann ever did any Pink Floyd translation but over tea and a lesson in drinking vodka straight we learned a few Polish jokes.

The best one, which I did not remember but Ann reminded me of years later, was this: 10 Russian men like to play Russian Roulette. There are 10 barrels. One is loaded. One man dies. 10 English men play roulette with glasses of Scotch. One is poison, one man dies. 10

Frenchmen play with 10 girls. One is diseased, one man dies. 10 Poles tell jokes. One is a KGB agent, 9 die.

There was a party going on down the hall. They invited us to come and dance. We also tried our first *bigos*. This was also known as the "hunter's stew", and it consisted of red meat, originally game, with fresh cabbage, *sauerkraut*, potatoes, wine sauce and I am not sure what else. It was rich, think, savory, heavy food, typical of the Polish cuisine.

A guy named Reszek offered Ann a dance, then another, then another and gave her a kiss on the hand after each one. Ann could not believe it, she thought she had gone back to the XIX century.

At the same party we met a smiling and exhilarating lady called Marta. She did not really study at our university, or at any other university for that matter, but was a friend of a friend of a student, or a cousin or something. Anyway she made her way into the party and was unabashedly on the prowl for a western boyfriend.

Most students were very happy to talk to us and their favorite topic of conversation was the Russians. Most (all?) just loathed the Russians and resented the system that the Soviet Union had imposed on Poland.

One guy was nicknamed Arbuz, which in Polish means "water melon", perhaps the most intriguing nickname I have ever heard of in any language or culture. He was drunk and could not really speak enough English to carry on a conversation. But he spent a good half hour spitting repeatedly on the ground while yelling: "Russki" and then stepping on his spittle. Even though we had no language in common that was communication enough.

Marta who claimed to be a little *Kommunistka* (communist youth) kept using the full force of her little body to shut him up. She said loud and clear for everyone to hear that "The Polish are a free people and can speak freely of many things. But there are some things about which one does not speak loudly about." And one was not supposed to spit on in public, I guessed.

24 February 1980 – Duck and wine

Our first Sunday in Poland rolled away smoothly. We got up late and drove to the *Stare Miasto* in search for a good meal but it was not so easy as many restaurants were closed.

After some walking around in the wintery Polish weather we ran into a pleasant small restaurant and took our seats. Using what little Polish we knew (Ann actually got by pretty well since she had been studying over the last few months and her family was originally from Poland and Slovakia, where they speak a similar language) we asked for the menu, but there was none. We then asked what was available, and the answer from the waiter was succinct and unmistakable: *kaczka*, ie duck.

OK so we ordered a delicious duck and some nondescript red wine. Duck was a pretty popular dish in Poland, and it will become a regular presence on our table. For the three of us the bill was 750 złoty (less than 7 dollars).

Before heading home I saw some painters in the square and bought two watercolors of the *Stare Miasto*.

Back in the male dorm we learned from our classmates that Marta the little communist girl had come looking for us and said hello… the first of many times she would make it clear to both Andrew and me that she was interested in at least one of us.

25 February 1980 – No *amatriciana* today

Full day at school and homework then out again for dinner at Ewa's. I had planned to cook spaghetti *amatriciana*, which I always execute following the traditional recipe very strictly: *guanciale*, *pecorino* (sheep milk cheese), no garlic, no onion especially, no carrot. But none of us was able to find anything resembling *guanciale*, the typical cured ham from Amatrice, nor bacon, which could have been an acceptable surrogate under the circumstances. Not even Ewa with all her black market connections.

Anyway we cooked some spaghetti and had a great time, eating away while engaging in another interminable conversation on the "real" Polish economy, and how to survive in it, or how to by-pass its structures and strictures to improve one's lot.

27 February 1980 – Mechanics and meat-free Wednesdays

After our morning classes we met Marian, who had promised to come over and help us find a mechanic to fix a dent in Giallina I had caused when I hit a curb in Vienna. He approached us from behind and kissed Ann on the hand! She still could not believe the gallantry of Polish men!

However, on our way to the garage, as we were jumping a curb to park on the sidewalk as is done in Poland, the wire that connects the accelerator pedal to the engine broke. We rigged the engine to drive in 1st gear to the garage. The mechanic, who ran a small shop, was able to fix Giallina with little difficulty, proving my theory that this old-style car, built with basic but sound components, was the right choice for this trip.

Meanwhile we got Marian to teach us another lesson number in the Polish economy. Today's topic: the police. He said "If police stop you, o.k., make private, make it off the record. If police try to give you a bill, you say, o.k., here is 500 złoty for you. Police only care about their own pocket." We had to laugh about what a sly, cool character he was. We spoke about laundry and he said, "o.k, I fix it for you, fast delivery: not 3 days, but 1 day, o.k.?" Present Marian with a problem and everything will be "o.k."

For dinner we decided to try the *Shanghai* restaurant, a Chinese joint on the Marszałkowska avenue, one of the main thoroughfares of the city. There were not many Chinese restaurants in Warsaw in 1980. In fact this is the only one I ever saw. China and Poland were both Communist countries of course, but Poland was officially a Soviet ally and China, after Mao's death, was edging closer to the West. Deng Xiaoping, the new leader who emerged from the power struggle that followed the Chairman's passing, famously visited Washington last year, in a historic first that paved the way for improved relations with the West in many areas.

We tried to order several meat dishes but after repeated denials by the waiter we were told that there was no meat today because it was Wednesday.

At the time we did not understand, but later on our Polish friends told us that, for some reason that I still do not understand, there was not supposed to be meat in any restaurant on Wednesdays. Why? I might have understood if Catholic Poland did not serve meat on Fridays, but why Wednesdays? We heard unconfirmed stories that the government was promoting meat-free Wednesdays to cope with scarce supplies of meat while officially masquerading the initiative as a measure to promote health.

In reality, Poles did eat a lot of fatty meat, and a bit less cholesterol might have been a good idea. However, we suspected the real reason for the cut back in proteins was economic: meat was expensive and Poland could not afford to produce enough of it, let alone import it. Actually it was exporting some, I had bought good Polish cooked ham in Washington, the government badly needed hard currency to pay its debts.

28 February 1980 – Another duck

After our daily classes at SGPiS we drove again to the *Stare Miasto* for lunch and tried a new small and unremarkable restaurant. One of many such restaurants in downtown Warsaw, where we felt welcome and somehow often ended up being the focus of their attention. Not too many western students showed up in a yellow Volkswagen Beetle I guess.

There were quite a few tourists in Poland these days, from both socialist and capitalist countries, but often they came in organized groups, and ate at more official establishments pre-organized through the state tourism board. Usually these were sterile restaurants in hotels without character.

We tried and ordered a number of different offerings from the menu, but the only available dish was... duck! We saw other people around us, all eating duck, we had not noticed at first but now it was clear that this was the thing to do. It was actually quite good and (for us) dirty cheap. We would come back fairly often to what will be remembered as our "duck place".

29 February 1980 – Socialist salaries

Today, after an economics class that touched on the issue of wages, we reflected a bit on socialist salaries. In just a few days in the country we heard a number of times that a manual worker, say in construction, or in a factory, earned more than an intellectual, say a professor, or a lawyer.

The reason that we were given was that the intellectual already got a lot of non-monetary satisfaction from his job, while the worker did not. Therefore it was only fair the worker should make more money. So an engineer made, on average, something around 6,000 zl per month, while a worker could expect about 10,000 zl. A very bizarre logic indeed but one that reflected the official ideology, and reality.

We heard, but could not verify first hand, that a farmer could expect to make less than either workers or intellectuals. And yet there was a scarcity of many agricultural products in the cities, so you would think farming would pay well. But it did not, though presumably farmers would be spared the trouble of standing in lines for hours to buy food.

Yet, many bright students competed for access to "intellectual" professions. Maybe because one does not live of bread alone. Or maybe because they thought this would open a door to emigrating to countries where their talents would be better rewarded. Hard to say.

The three of us went around town for errands. Ann was suffering terribly from a cold and ended up falling asleep on my bed. At 6 in the afternoon, little Marta dropped by and we dragged her with us to a concert, to which we couldn't get tickets anyway. She took us to a little night club. We treated her to wine and drove her to her apartment off a street called Puławska. After which Andrew felt like going out to socialize at a joint called *Sudoła*, while Ann and I called it a day.

1 March 1980 – Party in the girls' student dormitory

In the evening another party at the girls' dorm. One of an endless series of such parties we would attend during our stay in Poland, improvised on the flimsiest of excuses. One of our classmates would come forward and say: "Today it's my uncle's birthday!" or "my cousin's promotion, my parents' wedding anniversary... let's celebrate." Anything was a good justification to open a bottle of vodka and gobble up a few *kanapki*. These were small open sandwiches topped with pickles, tomatoes, and the inevitable *kiełbasa* (pronounced keeoohbàhsa, a popular type of fatty sausage), cheese, and anything else that happens to be at hand.

Fun company, not so much politics in tonight's conversation, which was unusual. Somehow our presence here in Poland was permeated by politics. For one thing, we came to study politics, and economics, so it went without saying that we would be interested in the subject and would bring it up often. Moreover, we came from the capitalist and democratic west to the socialist countries with their planned economies, which were supposedly working to build the utopian egalitarian communist society of the future. Or so the official saying went.

In reality, no one, not us and certainly not them, believed it. But whatever we did or talked about, politics and economics usually entered the discourse. There was much to compare and contrast between the two systems. Whether we were trying to buy something to eat, or fuel for Giallina, rent a hotel room, watch a movie, or go to a concert, the comparison was always between how they did it in the socialist, planned economy way, and how we did it the capitalist, or market way.

The crucial issue was our respective understanding of democracy. Democracy of course meant two different things. For us it meant free and unfettered elections, institutional checks and balances, freedom of expression, private property, rule of law.

For them, at least officially, it meant dictatorship by the proletariat, through a strictly centralized single party. This was the result of a revolution that would bring about a better world for everyone, not just the proletariat but the whole society. Several socialist countries had the word "democratic" or "people's" (which means the same thing really) in their official name. So Poland was really the Polish People's Republic, as was Hungary. East Germany was the German Democratic Republic.

Come to think of it, I was not able to recall a single democratic (our understanding of the word) country which had deemed it necessary to include that word in its official name of the state.[5]

But every single time we had such a conversation I had the clear impression that our Polish colleagues agreed with our interpretation of the word "democratic". I would never meet a single real believer in the socialist interpretation of democracy during all of my stay in Poland. Not one. (Ann did on a few occasions, which I am sorry I missed!)

---

5   *Years later I remember meeting a diplomat from Hungary just after the revolutions of 1989, when power reverted from the Party to the people. He gave me a business card, but they had not yet made new ones after the collapse of the socialist system. The card read "Hungarian People's Republic", but the word "People's" was crossed out!*

I actually felt kind of sad about it. I was not a socialist myself but felt that the ideals of socialism could be useful to guide an enlightened capitalist system toward greater fairness and compassion. But the Poles were too disillusioned with any kind of socialism to care about ideals any more.

The fatty sausages, hearty bread and all that cheese absorbed vodka to a surprising degree, but there was a limit. That limit was lower for us than for our Polish friends, who were much better trained at spirits and fatty food. By midnight or so Andrew and I were more than a bit tipsy but everything remained under control!

We talked a lot to Elżbieta tonight, she was actively helping in preparing the food. She was a quiet, soft spoken lady whom I will remember for a heart-shaped decal on her glasses. Her friend Bonga was very different, exuberant, hard laughing.

Marta was again on the offensive: tonight she tried her full arsenal of tricks to get into my bed, or Andrew's for that matter, and only gave up in the wee hours of the morning.

2 March 1980 – Fortune teller and full churches

Got up around 9 and at 10 we went for lunch with Marian and Ewa, together with her brother, father and sister in law. They recommend a restaurant outside Warsaw, on the road to Katowice, called *Mak*. We bought some "black" gasoline on the way, by now it had become pretty much routine.

Ewa's father was a peculiar character and offered to read the palms of our hands. He started to blurt out a number of our personal character traits with surprising accuracy. He said we should not take him too seriously, he was just an old man telling jokes. I am always very skeptical of this kind of skills, and would remain so, but I had to admit he got a lot right about us.

He told Ann she would attain a position of influence in life through her intelligence. In general, he said she was cautious, but at times threw all caution aside and pursued what her passions dictated. Finally he saw in her a person very sensitive to the pain of others, a person who cannot bear to see others wounded in any way.

In me he found a more stubborn character, a strong willed person who refuses to listen to the dictates of others when his conscience dictates otherwise. He saw me as an idealist who, although he will never realize his ideals, will achieve great monetary successes and will live a life full enough to satisfy more than one person.

I was perplexed when he also said I somehow looked Chinese, or that I had something Chinese in me.[6]

In Andrew he saw a man endowed with great capabilities, but also many inhibitions. He encouraged Andrew not to be so cautious and to take more risks in life.

Marian was very happy because he had just obtained his passport so he could travel to western Europe and asked us to change some money. We were given the usual lecture on the "real" Polish economy, this time concentrating on the real estate market.

It came in handy because I was looking for a short let for when my parents would come and visit us from Italy in the Spring. Of course it was not allowed for Poles to just rent a privately owned apartment (of which there were not too many) out to foreigners. However, this kind of capitalist profit making, like many other kinds of small scale private business, was widely tolerated.

At least Poles were allowed to own real estate, which was not the case is some other socialist countries. He said that OK, he would ask around and see what he could do. He loved to say OK whenever a question or a problem was laid before him, and that usually meant he had the answer, or the solution.

Marian also told us a lot about the international trade in Polish furs. Minks, mostly, but others as well, plus some more expensive kinds imported from the Soviet Union. Like many other things, these were cheap in Poland, if you could get a hold of them, and could command a considerable profit when sold in the West.

As we drove around on this easy Sunday we noticed a number of packed churches, with crowds of faithfuls overflowing outside the door. Catholicism was a deeply rooted tradition in Poland, we knew that, but this was surprising. We were told that rallying around the Church was the only (legal and unobjectionable) way to demonstrate political opposition to the regime. This was true even though the Church had come to a number of inevitable compromises with the Communist regime. Or, perhaps, precisely *because* it had.

In the late afternoon Ann went to visit some family on her father's side. They told her stories of the war, how all photos were

---

6   *In retrospect he was obviously referring to my future, to my yet-to-be-born Chinese wife, and in that case, again, he was right.*

destroyed by the Germans, about the reason why her grandfather left Poland (he didn't want to serve in the Russian army when Poland was part of Russia). One of millions of stories of Polish families caught, like their country, in the geographical vice of Germany to their west and Russia to their east.

Her uncle brought out a picture of her grandfather and she saw his eyes light up as he talked about what a wonderful person her grandfather was. She told me she looked into the young face of the person who was her grandfather and very eerily saw some of her own features.

For me it was a quiet evening at home, reading, writing, talking to Andrew as we began to draw our first political, economic and social conclusions from what we had experienced so far during the first couple of weeks of our semester here. Which was far more than we expected when we made up our mind to come to Poland over that lunch at the GU cafeteria last autumn.

3 March 1980 – A plateful of bison

In the afternoon we went to a public reading room. There were some international newspapers available for free, in several languages. Under a large sign that read "NEWSPAPERS FROM CAPITALIST COUNTRIES" there were two-week old copies of two italian dailies. One was *l'Unità*, the official paper of the Italian Communist Party. The latter had developed a different kind of Communist ideology than that of the Soviet Union, though it had never completely broken free. It professed to accept western-style democracy but never repudiated Marx. It was living in a difficult limbo.[7]

The other was *La Stampa,* a newspaper owned by the Agnelli family, a rich clan from Turin which also owned FIAT, the Italian car company that had been making huge investments in factories in Poland since 1932. In 1980 the unimaginatively renamed *Polski FIAT* was building its tiny 126 model. The Agnellis were the most powerful capitalists in Italy, the nemesis of Italian trade unions, and among the

---

7   *The Italian Communist Party, that had aspired to lead the communist movement toward democracy, actually <u>followed</u> Poland's and other eastern European brother parties to finally abandon the old ideology, and change its name, in 1991, two years after the upheavals that brought down the Soviet bloc.*

richest people in the world. Therefore they fully qualified as a top class enemy by definition, they should have been considered exploiters of the proletariat *par excellence*.

I was surprised. But they were spending money in Poland, transferring some technology and helping exports – some of the 126s were sold to other socialist countries and not a few even sent back to Italy. So their paper made it to the public reading room.

I supposed it all made sense, in a perverted sort of way. It would be the only Italian newspaper available during all my stay in Poland, at least that I could find, and therefore a precious source of relatively up-to-date information on my country, so I devoured its pages whenever I could.

There were actually a lot of cars in Poland, at least in the big cities. It was much easier to get hold of one, even if just a basic FIAT model, than, for example, in East Germany, where the wait was measured in decades! I was told of East Germans reserving a car when their child was born so that he could have it when he turned 18. It was not a joke, it really happened.

Later on in the afternoon Marta once again came to knock at the door of our male dorm room and tried various moves on Andrew and me. Again without success, though we admired her determination.

I then went to the post office to call Rome. We had no telephone in our room. We had one in the dorm but no international connection, for which we needed to go and try our luck at the post office every time. It usually worked.

I had a funny conversation with my brother Fabio when I tried to let him have our address: *Ulica Niepodległosci* (Independence Avenue), (pronounced something like Nee-ehpodlehgwòshchee) and when he asked for a spelling I could just utter "you write it as you read it, Polish is a phonetic language"! As if it were the most obvious for an Italian to understand Polish pronunciation with four hard consonants in a row over a decrepit phone line.[8]

Later on we had a chat with Stefan, a fellow student who was also a leader of the youth organization of the Communist party. He was a smart, articulate and very reasonable guy, not at all fanatic and actually highly critical of the Russians. We had yet to find one single

---

8   *As I am rewriting my notes for this book, in 2018, my brother still does not miss an opportunity to make fun of me because of this, and he is right!*

really dedicated Polish Communist in fact. We would become close friends with Stefan over the coming months.

In the evening we went for dinner to *Bazyliszek*, one of the best restaurants in town, located in the basement of picturesque building. The name comes from a legendary king of evil serpents, Basilisk, who lived in a basement in central Warsaw and had the power to kill with his ferocious glance anyone who would dare to go down to look at him straight in the eyes. The monster was eventually killed by a shrewd shoemaker who dressed himself up in a body armor of mirrors and went down, so that when the serpent looked at him it was killed by its own weapon. At least this is the story that is credited at the restaurant.

Bazyliszek was another memorable Epicurean experience and for the first time in my life I ate bison steak. A sumptuous meal set the three of us back by 1,300 złoty (12 dollars) including wine and it was unlikely we would ever be able to spend more very often for a fine dining meal Warsaw. I had no idea that there were bison in Europe, but there were, in the Bialowieza forest[9] of Poland, considered the oldest continuously alive forest of Europe, and a UNESCO World Heritage Site since 1979.

To celebrate Georgetown's basketball Championship victory, we stood on a bench in the Old Town Square and sang Georgetown's fight song. I am not sure anyone paid any attention to us among the few people we saw, but if they did we must have struck them as being as quite odd! It went like this:

> It's been so long since last we met
> Lie down forever, lie down
> Oh, have you any money to bet
> Lie down forever, lie down!
>
> There goes old...Georgetown
> Straight for a...touchdown
> See how they...gain ground
> Lie down forever, lie down

---

9 *As I looked at the website of Bazyliszek almost 40 years later, they no longer had bison on the menu. However they had Argentinian beef and Norwegian salmon.* Panta rei, *everything changes. (They still had duck though, of course!) Bison were still alive and kicking in the forest.*

Lie down forever, lie down!

Rah! Rah! Rah!
Hurrah for Georgetown
Cheer for victory today
'Ere the sun has sunk to rest,
In the cradle of the west
In the clouds will proudly float the Blue and Gray.

4 March 1980 – Ann is locked up in the boys' dorm

At school we told one of our professors that we had bison steak last night, we said we were impressed with the taste and texture. He was shocked, he said they had estimated that there were only seven bison left in the Masurian lakes, it was a highly endangered species. "Oh well" I replied as Ann tried to repress her laughter "there are only six now!"

In the afternoon we drove to the Praga district of town to deliver two letters on behalf of some American friends of Andrew's. No success, maybe we had the wrong address, but we could not find the people to whom the letter was written. Shame. We walked around a bit, curious as always to explore a new part of town, away from the beating heart of commercial activity and tourist attractions. It was a desolate, dark place. Piles of mud in the streets, dirty slush everywhere. This was not a fun part of town that we would be coming back to often, I thought on our way back. But then someone told us that, once a week, there was a farmers' market here and one could find all kinds of delicacies, including Russian caviar. I guess we will be back after all.

After that we went to *Hortex*, an eatery serviced by a large food company, and had a good fruit salad with ice-cream and walnuts for 46 złoty.

The three of us spent a quiet evening in our dorm room, chatting and having a light dinner. Around midnight, when it was time for Ann to leave and go back to her dorm, we realized all of our dorm's access doors to the street had been locked for the night! No way to get out of the building, not even an emergency exit. The window of our room was not an option either, as we lived on the third floor. But this being Poland, we knew there would be a way.

After looking around the ground floor lobby for a bit we found the room where the night porter was supposed to work. She was in fact sound asleep but not surprised to see us. An American quarter (a 25 US cents coin) to the chubby, cranky and drowsy porter lady finally bought Ann the freedom to walk back to her own female dorm a few hundred meters away, across Independence Avenue.

This procedure would be used quite frequently in the coming months: to get back into our dorm late after night out, to get out of our dorm and drive to a late party somewhere in town, and also to let our guests in and out the dorm after hours. Every time the chubby lady would get up, stagger to the door, open it and then drag herself back to her night station. There was no need to speak, she knew what to do and we knew what she expected in return.

5 March 1980 – Palace of Culture and Science

After our usual morning classes we went again for lunch in the university's cafeteria. We did not go there often, because it was so cheap for us to go to proper restaurants. But we did go to meet colleagues and enrich our experience as real Warsaw university students. We were unavoidably special, but did not want to be too special, we tried to mingle with our colleagues.

After a forgettable meal I went back to the post office to call my family in Rome. By now I was getting used to not having a private phone at "home", not to call and not to receive calls. There was a collective telephone in the hallway of our dorm, and sometimes we would arrange to receive calls there, but you had to (literally) stand by to pick it up when it rang or be lucky that someone else would pick it up for you and knock at your room's door to alert you of the incoming call.

Dad and mum would be coming to visit next month, and were getting ready with air tickets, visas, dollar bills etc. I was quite happy they were coming, I enjoyed making them part of our experience. And they loved Andrew and Ann as well. Whenever possible my parents would come visit in many places where I traveled around the world: they had come to the United Kingdom when I was studying English at Bournemouth, they had come to Washington to see Georgetown, and now wanted to fly to Poland, a destination that otherwise might not have been at the top of their "to-do list" but that they would end up loving beyond expectations. Every time they showed interest in everything I was doing, but they were never invasive of my private spaces and time. I was lucky.

Andrew and I then went downtown for a walk. Our target today was the *Pałac Kultury y Nauki* (Palace of Culture and Science). Highly controversial for some time, it had become a permanent fixture of the Warsaw skyline. It was a "gift" (read: "imposition") from the Soviet Union at the time of Stalin. It had been designed by the famous Soviet architect Lev Rudnev as a copy of seven buildings in Moscow, dubbed "Stalinist skyscrapers", and conceived to celebrate the greatness of the supreme leader with majestic shapes that reminded one of the Gothic towers pointing to the sky, and to God.

During a couple of hours inside the palace we did not find much that looked special or that we could really appreciate. However I actually kind of liked the architecture itself of the Soviet skyscraper, though it was easy to understand how every single Pole we talked to saw is as a symbol of Soviet domination and therefore resented its imposing intrusion into their capital's skyline.

In the evening Ann went out with a guy called Wadim, brother of one of her roommates, who fancied her a lot. Andrew and I decided to rest in our dorm room. We were afraid Marta would show up and prepared a line of defense: we would pretend we had to study.

After a while, however, Andrew got bored and decided to go and check out the *Hades* bar/café our friends had recommended. There he found a concert, fun music to listen to but very noisy so not much of a chance to talk to other students or pick up a girl! I stayed put and read a book, luckily Marta did not materialize.

7 March 1980 – Credit, Beethoven and bear steak

Usual classes in the morning, it was routine by now and our professors were not as interesting as they could have been because they were politically constrained in what they were allowed to say, but we never skipped class anyway. We were learning to decipher their lectures through the colored lenses of ideology, and that would be a learning experience in itself.

At 5:00pm we listened to a lecture by a Polish professor on "East-West Trade", ie commerce between the capitalist countries of western Europe and north America and the socialist bloc of eastern Europe. He said nothing unpredictable: we needed to increase the value of East-West trade, we needed to raise the volume of exchanges. Nice in principle except but he must have been well aware that Polish products were difficult to sell in the West. He also asked for more "cheap credit" from the West to finance Polish purchases of western product. Right.

Well, not completely surprising: by 1980 Poland was running out of cash. During the 1970s Gierek's government has been splurging to keep people happy but by now the coffers were empty. Lacking market reforms, cheap external credit was the only way for the regime to survive. I asked him how Poland could increase productivity and thus afford to pay back its growing international debts in hard currency, but he was rather evasive. Of course he was: the only way would have been to introduce market reforms, private enterprises, foreign capital, and other such ideologically unacceptable reforms.

Moreover, Poland, like other socialist countries, was getting subsidies from the USSR, both in the form of cheap energy and with the Soviets buying Polish exports that no one else was interested in. Moscow did this to keep its satellite states from developing social problems which might endanger its political control on the region. But it was not enough, Poland was not rich by any stretch of the imagination yet it was still living beyond its means.

In the evening great concert by the Austrian pianist Rudolf Buchbinder. The three of us managed to get really good seats (second row for only 60 złotys). It was an all-Beethoven program, including the *Appassionata*, one of my favorites sonatas for solo piano.

After the concert we went for dinner at the *Canaletto* restaurant of the Victoria hotel and, to properly follow up on the bison steak of two days ago, for the first time in my life I ate a steak of bear meat! I certainly did not expect these culinary surprises in Poland but thoroughly enjoyed them both and was looking for the next one. Delicious. Only 1500 złotys (about 13 dollars) for the three of us and this in one of the most expensive restaurants in the city.

As we savored our steaks we reasoned that this system could not work. The currency was grossly overvalued at the official exchange rate. Of course Poles could not buy dollars with their złoty so they had to spend them at home but because productivity was low there was not enough to buy. Shelves were either empty or stacked with second rate goods nobody wanted. Therefore Poles were happy to dump heaps of złoty on foreigners in order to get a few dollars to use abroad or in the *Pewex* special stores.

At the other extreme, those with dollars, ie us foreigners and a few privileged ones like athletes, diplomats, and of course illegal traders and smugglers, enjoyed a black market rate so favorable that it made everything available on the local market so cheap, too cheap.

Other privileged ones, who did not necessarily have money but had access to special supply chains, included high-ranking members of the Communist Party, or of the Church for that matter. Something had to give. Most people were cut off from this bonanza but they were painfully aware of the situation and were unlikely to put up with it for long.

The day ended with a long talk in the car with Ann, until about 3:00am. We talked about what we were experiencing. Poles had risen against the Communist system already in 1956 and again more recently, in 1976, only to be crushed by the security forces under threat of invasion by Moscow. We thought they were likely to do so again, though there was nothing we saw or heard that suggested this would be imminent.[10]

More importantly, we agreed that once they did rise, they would be crushed again, by their own military or by the socialist brother countries of the Warsaw Pact, or both. That would be painful for Poland and it might also create ripples of instability in all of Europe.

So I told Ann that personally, and perhaps a bit selfishly, I hoped they would not rise: I feared the resulting repression would not benefit Poland and it might endanger our way of life in western Europe, even provoke a war between the blocs. There was only so much a proud nation like Poland could swallow before saying that enough was enough.

---

10 *We were wrong: the Solidarity movement, which marked the decisive rebellion of Poland against communism, began in August 1980, just weeks after the end of our program in Warsaw.*

8 March 1980 – Concert and women's day with Polish girls

Woke up late, around noon, for a lazy Saturday. Ann and I went for lunch to the hotel *Forum*, one of the poshest in Warsaw.[11] It was a well known retreat for foreigners and the Polish elite, but it was nothing special, we were a little disappointed for its price level. The hotel itself was very modern, it had been designed by Swedish architect Sten Samuelson and built at record speed (so they told us) just six years ago. It was the second tallest building in Warsaw after the Palace of Culture and Science.

During lunch Ann told me how, because today it was International Women Day, she had spent the morning in the dorm with Alina and Elżbieta "waiting for gifts". Apparently that is a Polish tradition she found rather flattering. Several male friends and acquaintances had come by to drop their best wishes and their XIX century gallantry. So she dumped me for the day.

She later told me how in fact they received cards, gifts and flowers, which made her feel quite flattered and happy, especially because she realized this was probably going to be the only time in her life she would be on the receiving end of such effusive generosity and courtship.

In the evening I was invited by Christopher, a Pole I met at school, to attend another concert at the Chopin Society, the same venue as yesterdays' concert. Again a Buchbinder recital but this time he played Schumann and Beethoven.

Christopher spoke perfect English and German and was eager to talk to westerners. Of course, for all we could tell, he might be working for the Communist party and could have been tasked with testing our views and monitoring our movements and contacts. We'll never know for sure.

Come evening Andrew and I went to the *Stodoła* (The Barn) where we picked up three Polish girls and spent the rest of the evening with them, ending up at the *Bazyliszek* restaurant for some ice-cream. We completely forgot it was International Women's Day so we did not proffer any effusive poetry to the poor girls.

I have a habit of forgetting anniversaries and birthdays and the like for the people I care about, and am even worse for official

---

11 *It would become part of the Novotel chain in 2002.*

celebrations. Surely they must have been disappointed in their heart but we had a good time together nonetheless.

It was always difficult to tell how much the local girls we met were interested in us just like any college kid the world over is interested in a date or if it was the fact that we were from the "rich" capitalist west that attracted their attention. I came to the conclusion that was a mix of both in most cases.

We were all normal students after all, even though we were more than a bit exotic as there were so few of us from the "West", and they enjoyed going out on a date just like students everywhere. But the prospects of a good and otherwise unaffordable meal and perhaps a trip or even a move to our side of the (iron) curtain definitely played a role some of the time, and for some of them this was a decisive role.

9 March 1980 – Churches in Warsaw

Despite our firm lack of any religious belief whatsoever, Andrew and I decided to go and have a look at a church downtown in order to witness first hand the reality of Catholicism in Poland.

The church was packed to the brim with people. In fact the crowd overflowed out of the building and many of the faithful listened to the Mass from outside. We were of course aware that Poland was a very Catholic country, and of how this peculiarity had produced a complex situation.

On the one hand, the official top hierarchy of the catholic Church had found a *modus vivendi* with the communist government, and enjoyed more freedom than in other socialist countries.

On the other hand, it remained one of the few channels through which dissent could be expressed, if cautiously. For one thing, churches were among the few places where large numbers of people were still free to congregate in large numbers and talk among themselves without asking for a permit and without fear of arrest.

The election of the Polish cardinal from Krakow to the top of the Holy See a year and a half ago had galvanized the nation and had provided a ray of hope for its opposition to Soviet control. Last year pope John Paul II had made a triumphant visit back in his home country. One of the open-air masses he celebrated attracted a crowd that was estimated at a mind boggling three million people in and around Victory Square in central Warsaw. Never had a gathering of the communist party come even close to these numbers. I wished I had been there to witness it, you could still hear the reverberations of the chants of that memorable day in June 1979.

10 March 1980 – Yet another duck, the moon and the stars

After our usual morning classes we went for lunch at another "duck place", which we found was called the restaurant *Kmicic*. We ate our usual *kaczka*. Somehow there was never want of ducks on Warsaw's restaurant plates.

In the evening we all went to a party at the home of a certain Leszek, curiously nicknamed Dyndol. Lots of friendly people in attendance, while *kanapki* and vodka abounded all around us. Maybe because of the latter, after a while some people started behaving funny. A certain Jan set up a barricade of furniture for the purpose of cornering Ann in the room and making clear his predilection for her. This despite the fact that he was married, his wife Bożena (pronounced Bawjehna) was pregnant and everyone else at the party was aware of this. Several friends also whispered, with a mix of suspicion and caution, that Jan was working for Polish intelligence services, which made it even more startling that he behaved the way he did!

I tried to make some sense of this hitherto unheard of (to me) behavior but Alina explained to me that this was normal: "Jan is used to Bożena", she said, and "therefore it is natural for him to be looking for fun with other women". All Poles did this, especially men but also women, she explained matter-of-factly, once they "got used" to their partner, and they made no apologies for it.

I would hear this story on a number of occasions in the next couple of months. Apparently it was standard operating procedure. I supposed no harm was done as long as everyone was aware of the rules of the game and accepted them.

As the evening progressed Ann, who had managed to extricate herself from Jan's furniture barrier, became a bit confused when Wadim showed up and promised her "the moon and the stars" if she finally agreed to accept his insistent manifestations of love draped in XIX century chivalry jargon. Well, how the matter was resolved between them I know not, but we all went home safe, though very

very late, the moon and stars remained high in the night sky and we were just a bit perplexed.

11 March 1980 - Mushrooms and cream

We were dead for classes, which was no great hardship since Bogdan took us down to the lounge and then the Polish Political Systems professor, Dorota Gierecz, took us out for coffee at a nearby café called *Zielona Ges* (Green Goose). Academic life here was really demanding! We were taking classes in a coffee shop!

Ann said she was not getting much formal studying of Polish done. Too much traffic in her quadruple girls' room. The four of them were popular and received many guests and suitors!

To confirm that, in the evening, Bonga had promised to make us her special *pieczarki w smietanie* (mushrooms with cream), so we all gathered together in the evening over a bottle of wine to sample this Polish specialty, which was very tasty indeed. We would order it repeatedly at various restaurants, but the home made version by Bonga would stay in our hearts.

12 March 1980 – Car wash, passport photos and cold broth

After a history class Ann and I went to the Victoria restaurant anticipating a good steak, they were well known for their *Chateaubriand* – the thick part of filet mignon – apparently so named after a French diplomat of the XIX century who apparently had an especially soft spot for this cut. After we parked the car two rather destitute men asked whether we would like Giallina washed by hand while we had our meal. I declined, she was clean enough. Besides, they asked for three dollars, while on another occasion, when we were with Polish friends, the rate was only one dollar and a half, so they were clearly doubling the price for foreigners and I did not appreciate that.

As we walked into the restaurant we realized that the *Canaletto* restaurant was closed, and the second restaurant of the hotel, the *taverna*, did not have *Chateaubriand* on the menu. We had a good lunch anyway. As we were about to leave our waiter came over and unabashedly asked us to change money, but we did not, not knowing the guy. It could be a rip off or worse, a trap to embarrass foreign capitalists, you never knew, and anyway we had our trusted contacts.

As we walked away from the restaurant to the parking lot a taxi drove by and the driver also asked to change money, and we again declined. Back to our car, we found that the two men I had turned down had cleaned our car anyway! Well, I gave them 200 złoty, the "local" car cleaning rate, and they seemed happy after all.

I then went with Ann to various tourist offices where we found no information at all in any language on Wroclaw, Gdansk or Lublin, three cities we wanted to visit over the next several weeks. Poland was clearly not geared up to welcome international tourism. Or domestic tourism, for that matter. It was all a do-it-yourself effort, but in a way that made it more fun and opened the door to a degree of serendipity that would enrich our experience further.

We then walked into a photographer's shop to get some passport size shots in anticipation for various visas we would be applying for in the near future. We got twenty-one very professionally finished black&white pictures each for only 71 złotys, less than a (black market) dollar. I was very happy with the result, it almost made me look like a handsome young man, the studio lighting was perfect, the soft background contrasted well with my elegant trench coat and my smile was framed by gentle shadows around my cheeks and lips.

Several days later I would come back to this shop and had more photographs taken of me, anticipating that I would use them for my passports, driver's licenses, ID cards etc. for many years to come, to the point that by the time I ran out I hardly resembled the twenty year-old man, still sporting a considerable amount of hair on his head, who was pictured in them.

In the evening we dined with Marian and Ewa. Lots of pork and a special gelatinous sausage, kind of similar to Italian *coppa*. It had been made by Ewa herself and she served it to us with a savory cold broth. It was an unusual combination but a tasty and definitely a nutritious one.

Marian and Ewa again railed against the system and put forward several ideas for us to cooperate in making some money in the future, by selling in Italy some luxury products, mostly made in the USSR, that we could procure in Warsaw at cheap prices through their unofficial supply channels.

14 March 1980 – *Fusilli alla carbonara*

In the evening I went to the girls' dorm to cook pasta. For the occasion I invested in a 30-złoty aluminum pot of sufficient capacity. I also bought Polish pasta (*fusilli* to be precise), not without serious reservations (will they be made of durum wheat?) about its quality. I also bought eggs and bacon (the closest I could find to Italian *guanciale*) to make *carbonara*, one of my favorite cheap and cheerful pasta recipes. *Carbone* means coal, and while the etymology of the name is uncertain it may have something to do with the blackish look of fried pork fat chunks.

You panfry the bacon until crispy and then dry it on kitchen tissue to get rid of the excess fat. While you boil the pasta you can beat one egg per person plus one in a bowl. Some people prefer to only use the yolk, it will result in a denser creamier sauce. When the pasta is cooked (*al dente* of course) you drain it and drop it into the pan you used for the *guanciale* together with the crispy fat-deprived pork for about 30 seconds on slow fire to amalgamate them together. Then you turn off the stove and pour in the eggs and keep stirring. It's important the fire is off so the eggs stay liquid and do not coagulate much. Add some grated *pecorino* or *parmigiano* and serve immediately. When I was younger I used to add some milk or cream to make it taste smoother, and also because the girls I was trying to impress tended to like it better, but I gave up as it is not the real recipe.

The end result was actually pretty close to the real thing, and the girls liked it quite a lot! It was of course very different from any Polish recipes but *carbonara* suited the hearty and full body character of Polish cuisine, so I was not surprised our Polish friends loved it.

15 march 1980 – Warsaw Museum and lines for bread

In the morning the three of us went to the Warsaw Museum and watched a film on the systematic destruction of the city by the Nazi.[12] The first part of the film focused on the diabolically methodical approach to the destruction, the second part on the subsequent reconstruction after World War II.

---

12 *In 1983 they would establish the Warsaw Uprising Museum, fully dedicated to the tragedy of the city's uprising during the Nazi occupation.*

The Russians' contribution to the reconstruction took center stage in this very politically correct second part, which was highly propagandistic in nature. Most historians in the West argued that the Russians had their own fair share of responsibility in the destruction of the city. This is because they delayed its liberation from the eastern bank of the Vistula, where the Red Army waited for the Germans to finish their job before crossing over.

Others argue the Soviet lines were over-extended and they were in no position to move in sooner. Be that as it may, the hatred of Stalin for Poland, and for the Polish army in particular, was well known, and we will have further opportunities to talk about it later in our trip.

As we drove away we saw a long line of people, at least forty or fifty, queuing up for bread half the way around a block! Polish bread was always very good by the way, especially the dark whole wheat versions.

We then went for lunch at the *Habana* restaurant, which actually hardly anything Cuban to show. Cuba was, of course, a communist brother country, and Castro was officially considered a hero for standing up to the United States, but in realty few Poles knew much about Cuba, or cared.

In the evening Stefan came to talk in our room and told us how when he was attending official meetings (he was the president of the SGPiS student association) he was always kept apart from the Russians, as if the senior leaders of the two parties did not want their young ones to fraternize. He made no qualms of his growing disillusionment with the socialist big brothers.

16 March 1980 – *Łazenki*, old ghetto, change of the guard

Quite a full Sunday that started with a tour around town in the company of our new acquaintance Jurek and a hired guide, Stanisław. We first visited the *Łazenki* (pron: Wajehnkee) park, a mix of green lawn, neoclassic buildings and fountains. The larger than life Chopin monument was a permanent exhibit here. The Polish composer of intimate piano music remained a source of national pride, and rightly so, whatever the ideology of the government at any time in recent Polish history.

Afterwards we moved downtown and witnessed the very martial change of the guard at the monument of the unknown soldier. The Polish military were a proud bunch, and were living through a difficult time. They were formally allied with the Soviet Union as part of the military Pact that was signed in and named after their own capital city. For some Poles perhaps this was a kind of reassurance against a resurgent and remilitarized West Germany in NATO. For most however, in light of recent history and current politics, it was the Soviet Union that represented a threat to national self-determination.

No one we ever met had much good to say about the Soviet military and their permanent presence in Poland except for the fact that far greater numbers were present in East Germany and contributed to make sure the Germans (East or West) did not stir up trouble again. Poland had lost a lot of its eastern land to the USSR (and Soviet-occupied Lithuania) after World War II, but gained quite a chunk along its western border from Germany, so in a diabolic, twisted way the Soviets did perform a useful role for Poland.

Finally we walked around the old Jewish ghetto. There was an enormous monument to the victims of the Nazi repression there. The Polish ghetto was a bastion of resistance to the Nazis during the occupation of Warsaw, and paid a huge price in the fight for freedom. Polish Jews represented the largest group of victims in the German concentration camps.

A few people labored on the public gardens, it was an example of the so-called "Sunday voluntary work" instituted by the socialist regime to show the people's mutual solidarity and dedication to the common good. The look on their faces showed something less than unbridled enthusiasm for this extra unpaid chore, however.

In the evening we had dinner with Stefan and his girlfriend Ewa at the *Krokodyl* restaurant, one of the best in the old town. No one was able to explain the origin of the name, but apparently when Fidel Castro dined here in 1972 as part of his official visit to the socialist brother country of Poland he was so disappointed not to find any crocodile that he sent a stuffed one from Cuba as a gift.

Another superb meal in Warsaw, replete with red meat and good wines though no, they still did not have crocodile steak on the menu. I did feel a bit guilty about being able to splurge like this in the face of widespread penury of meat in the city. But not guilty enough to give it up! And it would not help anyone to give it up anyway. Our guilt was compounded by the fact that Stefan very generously insisted on paying for everyone.

17 March 1980 – Planning ahead: USSR and DDR

As one of our usual morning classes was cancelled we spent part of the morning and the afternoon touching base with the respective tourist offices and consulates to organize our upcoming trips to East Germany and the Soviet Union. It seemed we would have quite a lot of obstacles to overcome in both cases. In the case of East Germany the problem for us was essentially economic: they wanted to charge us, at a minimum, 55 US dollars per person, per day, for their cheapest hotel. So much for socialist solidarity with poor college students. We refused and started to consider alternative plans.

The case of the USSR was equally difficult because of cost: we had to go through the Polish state-run *Orbis* tourist agency, the only one allowed to co-operate with *Intourist*, the government travel agency in charge of all foreign tourism in the land of the socialist brothers of the Soviet Union. It was also complicated: the itinerary would have to be specified in advance and could not be changed.

They told us that apparently all western exchange students who had tried to organize individual itineraries (as opposed to pre-packaged tours) before us had been refused a visa. They told us our only hope was to join one of their all-inclusive groups where the western capitalists were bussed from one monument to another and back to their hotel without the slightest chance of seeing anything about the real life of the country, or talk to anyone besides the indoctrinated tour guides.

Of course we had not even considered that option. Despite the inevitable limitations of ANY trip to the USSR, we wanted to be as much as possible on our own, free to meet locals and explore out of the beaten path.

Marta again returned, undaunted and stubborn, to the male dorm to try her luck with me and Andrew. Thanks but no thanks.

Evening in Stefan's room with a few classmates. We all ate various cuts of cold meat, *kanapki*, red beans and peppers. The occasion was the birthday of some family member of one of them, but we did not really need an occasion. Not today nor for any other party we would share in the dorm. Everyone was so kind to us it was almost embarrassing. Even with those who didn't speak much English there was no problem of communication. We were, somehow, on the same wavelength, even though we had received a very different education and upbringing and had been exposed to wildly different political and economic experiences.

18 March 1980 – Hope for travel to the East

Another visit to Orbis gave us some hope that apparently, for some unfathomable reason, we were now likely to get an individual visa to the USSR. We met a certain Mr. Głembinski who had been recommended to us by a woman at the Soviet tourist agency Intourist. He said that we might be able to travel with Giallina and stay in various hotels and camping sites on our individually designed tour. We would have to decide on a fixed itinerary and not change it even a little bit after the visa was issued, but we were on!

Evening at the restaurant *Pod Gołębiami* (Under the Pigeons), pretty good and sooo inexpensive. We did not eat pigeon, it was not on the menu. I would have if it had been, but for some reason my American friends were horrified by the prospect of eating pigeons, they considered the birds disgusting.

19 March 1980 – Pasta and music

A pleasant day. We ate Italian spaghetti on Mokotowska street for lunch. My expectations were low but in fact the stuff was good even for a picky Italian like me!

In the evening Ann and I dragged Andrew to hear a violin and piano recital. The first two pieces, one by Tartini and the other by Brahms, somehow did not seem to us to harmonize the violin with the piano. However, after the intermission, Saint Saens was enjoyable and Paganini, as always, was impressive.

Warsaw has an excellent offer of classical music performances, a surprise for me. Also lots of theater, which for us is less interesting because of the language barrier. I have not seen many cinemas, but maybe it's just because I have not looked hard enough.

20 March 1980 – Class in Polish foreign policy

First lesson in Polish foreign policy. It was not held at the university but rather at a think tank run by the ministry of foreign affairs, the *Polski Institut Spraw Międzynarodowich* (Polish Institute of International Affairs or PISM).

Our teachers were all retired Polish diplomats. The tone of their lectures was very formal, official, stiff. While they were mostly likable and reasonable people, they stuck strictly to the party line. We got the definite feeling that they sometimes did not really believe what they were telling us. They had to recite the orthodoxy, which sometimes made sense. Most of the time it did not, but it was the only game in town in terms of a discussion on foreign policy.

For dinner we went to the hotel *Metropol*. A waiter asked us if we wanted to buy 600 grams of (obviously black market) Soviet caviar for 40 US dollars, a ridiculously cheap price anywhere in the West, and we pleaded the plight of the poor student to which he responded with the plight of the destitute waiter. We did not buy in the end, but we knew we would before long. My idea was to take some caviar back to Italy at the end of our stay and sell it at a profit. Or at least sell some of it at a profit and share the rest with family and friends. The waiter actually sang songs about wonderful America in Polish and waited around for his tip. When we left some change on the table he squealed, *"Dla mnie!"*, (for me!), like a little kid and gobbled it up. He was clearly very surprised. Poles were not big tippers it seemed.

21 March 1980 – Off to Lublin

After our usual morning classes at the Central School we were told we would have an extra, foreign policy class in the afternoon, which almost forced us to cancel the trip we had planned to Lublin.

The three of us went for lunch at the *Warszawa* hotel. We were not that hungry and ordered a few appetizers but for some reason each of us was served two portions. We asked why but, as by now we had learned through experience was often the case in Poland, there was no explanation, we just got to eat double sized appetizers today. After which we were more than satisfied even though left with our stomachs fuller than we had planned.

In the afternoon foreign policy classes at PISM for three and a half hours. Again, very official, rigid teaching by the professors who just pushed the party line with meticulousness but without zeal and no enthusiasm whatsoever. When we would put forward a politically sensitive question involving the USSR, they would smile and advise to ask Soviet president Brezhnev!

In the late afternoon we finally set off to Lublin with Giallina. The "highway" was pathetic: no guardrails, lots of potholes, bumps, narrow turns, a mess. Truck drivers made things worse by using their high-beams very liberally. In fact I had the definite impression that they did it on purpose, for the fun of making car drivers uncomfortable. It happens in Italy too, I was not as surprised as Ann and Andrew to suffer through this. A couple of times I risked an accident because I was totally blinded but in the end we got to Lublin in one piece.

Lublin was rather underwhelming and unimpressive. The old town had been restored after the extensive (to put it mildly) wartime damage, but still... too neglected, dirty. One of the few disappointments so far in this trip. It was a bit tricky to find a place to sleep. Of course we had made no bookings, and usually that was not a problem. The first hotel, the Victoria, was full.

The second, whose name was evidently so not worth noting that I forgot it, started making things unnecessarily complicated. First they wanted us to change dollars, which of course we would not do with strangers. Second they said if we did not have western money we would have to produce an official receipt to show that we had exchanged our Polish currency in a legal way.

Now for one thing we never changed legally, but in this case the request was rather preposterous as we, officially registered students at an accredited university, were allowed to pay in złoty with no further questions asked. Apparently though this only applied to cheap student hostels, not to good hotels where real people stayed. But the guy at the reception was being unreasonable. To make matters worse I had forgotten my passport in Warsaw so I could not prove who I really was. I had my pink canvas Italian driver license but somehow it was not enough. (I naively did not think one needed to carry a passport to travel within the country.)

In the end Andrew dug in his pockets and found some old receipt from a month ago or so when we had exchanged a few leftover Austrian schillings for złoty. It was an official receipt all-right, but for a small amount and not enough to cover the cost of the room for one night. The hotel guy, luckily, was not familiar with foreign exchange and did not verify the amount. As we grew increasingly exasperated, Andrew said: "Look. Here is the situation. We're here. Marco's passport is in Warsaw. We have to sleep somewhere. Do you want us to go out and spend the night in the car?" Finally the receptionist relented and let us in. However he insisted he could only check-in Andrew and Ann, not passportless me. So we booked a room for two people and in the end, after an hour drinking beer while watching locals getting wasted in the restaurant of the hotel, I smuggled myself in.

22 March 1980 – Lublin, Tartars and Lenin

The morning receptionist was more awake than his colleague the previous night and he discovered the schilling trick but Ann was able to produce another exchange receipt from the depths of her purse and everything was ok. We didn't bother to claim our breakfast and just got the hell out before they could think of something else to make our life difficult.

We spent the morning walking around the old town. For some reason there was not one single restaurant that was open for business. Also, most shops were closed so we could not buy a funnel, which we needed to fill our car's tank with the black market fuel we were rather dangerously carrying in various plastic tanks in the trunk. We had to make do without a funnel, which resulted in a minor spill of fuel, but nothing serious.

In the afternoon we drove to Sandomierz, where we contacted the family of Elżbieta, our colleague at SGPiS who was the resident *przewodnicząca* (a kind of student/administrator, or resident assistant, this was another Polish word I was never able to pronounce) in the *Sabinki* dorm with Ann. They had been told of our arrival and were extremely welcoming and of course had prepared an extensive meal with all kinds of delicacies for us.

A young lady called Ulla, a friend of the family, offered to show us around town. We visited the cathedral, gave us a guided tour in Polish which Ann translated for the benefit of Andrew and me. She pointed out the cathedral and the Romanesque Church, which an American wanted to buy and transport piece by piece to the states.

The walls of the church were largely covered with freaky paintings of horror scenes depicting the repeated Tartar invasions during the XIII century. People gutted alive, quartered, eviscerated. The friendliest treatment the Tartars apparently reserved for the locals was to behead them.

There were also some depictions of Jewish ritual murders of Christians. According to undocumented stories, called "blood libels", the Jews required blood, especially from Christians, to perform certain religious ceremonies at Passover. The existence of these macabre traditions was never proven but their alleged cruelty had been used to fuel antisemitism here and elsewhere. And this despite several popes (and a Sultan!) denouncing the practice, hence "libel" over several centuries. A bizarre church indeed.

After a while a friend of Ulla's showed up. He tried, unsuccessfully, to make a few moves on Ann, but then resigned himself to showing us around the Lenin museum, overflowing with images of the revolutionary leader during the various phases of his rocambolesque existence. Lenin sketched, Lenin painted, Lenin in black and white, Lenin's profile, Lenin with the workers, Lenin with the peasants, Lenin visiting Poland and even! We were the only visitors of the museum, of which fact for some reason I was not surprised.

After the exhibit, all the others went upstairs and Ann remained downstairs with the strange fellow who kissed her hand a dozen times, and told her to wait in that spot while he turned off the lights. Ann yelled "Marcoooo!" and I ran downstairs cursing at the maniac.

The last highlight of the day was a tunnel, about 420 meters long, that was used by the local population to hide from the Tartars. As we went to sleep it comes to mind that Lenin was of partial Tartar descent, but never mind.

Ulla had she reserved a room for us in a hotel in the square, the *Dom Turysty* (Tourist House) where she convinced the girl of our destitute situation and we had to pay only 200 złoty.

Again, Ann and Andrew had to sneak passportless me into the room. We were so exhausted that we fell asleep on the spot.

23 March 1980 – Elections for Parliament

We spent the morning walking about Sandomierz without any particular goal in mind. By lunch time we said goodbye to Elżbieta's family and Ulla, but not before we were treated to another Pantagruelian meal at her home, where we were also entrusted some packages to take back to Warsaw for her, some local gastronomic delicacies I think.

It so happened that today was election day in Poland. People were called to vote for the new Parliament, the *Sejm*. There were few political posters in Sandomierz, I guessed because there was no need to campaign, really. The outcome was well known in advance. One poster did exhort voters to participate nonetheless: "Support the party: vote!"

Just for fun, we went and had a look at a polling station. People walked in, we watched about fifteen, took their ballot and dropped it in a big box. No one went into a small booth that had been set up in a corner of the room to provide privacy to mark anything on the ballot. Not that there would be much choice. Only the Communist party and a few nominally independent but very subservient allied parties were allowed on the ballot. A blank ballot was taken as a vote for the list of communist-approved candidates printed on it.

Anyway, in Poland, Parliament's role was restricted to rubber stamping the Party's decisions. It was in the Party hierarchy that all meaningful political debate took place and decisions were taken. The executive, legislative and judiciary branches of government were stuffed with party appointees who took instructions from the Central Committee. No checks and balances, no rule of law. The Party was the law. It could make it, change it at will and push it down the administration's throat to be mechanically implemented.

We then set off to Kazimierz, a small medieval town nearby with a pretty castle on top of a steep hill. On the way we taught Ann how to drive a manual shift car, she had only ever driven automatic. She did pretty well for a beginner! We also used up our very last reserves of black market gas we had been carrying around in our illegal plastic containers. We spilled a little bit as we had no funnel.

Once at Kazimierz we climbed up the Hill of Three Crosses, on top of which we found ...three crosses and from which we could enjoy a great view of the town. It was very cold: spring formally started three days ago but there was little sign of it in Poland so far.

In the evening we drove back to Warsaw when we realized we were running out of gas and feared we wouldn't make it. We rolled into one gas station and he demanded official coupons. First, we tried to bribe him then Ann explained our situation in Polish. He hesitated, and then gave us enough gas to get to Warsaw. We respected him because he refused to be "bribed" and charged us as if we were Poles. We made it, by the way, just.

24 March 1980 – Expanding our collection of visas

After our usual morning classes we wanted a bite at the Ambassador Hotel across from the US embassy, but arrived half an hour before its official lunch hours. Furthermore, they were filming over and over one waiter serving a patron soup. They would cut the lights and film the same scene over again. We were about to leave the restaurant but were followed by the manager who told us they sometimes open early "for their guests". So we went back, sat down and watched twenty more times how they filmed the waiter serve that actor/patron soup.

After which we drove off to the Soviet consulate to see whether they had any news about our visa applications. They said there was still hope to get it but it was not yet there for us. We would have to go back one more time in a few days. No point trying to call, we would have to pick ourselves up and be there in person.

Then it was the turn of the Polish visa office. Why did we need another visa for Poland? Because if we did eventually go to the USSR, we would need to exit Poland, but then we would have to come back into the country on our way home. The current visa stamped on our passport was valid for one entry only. And in any case it was going to expire before we returned from the Soviet Union, because it was only meant to last until the end of our study program, and not for our extracurricular excursion to the East.

Finally it was the turn of the Orbis office, the Polish tourist agency where we had to prepare papers and photos for Cathy, a friend of Ann's back in the US who was supposed to join us for a post-semester tour.

By the end of the afternoon we had filled out a dozen forms in three different offices. And it was not over, they all told us to come back in a few days. Part of the "real" Polish experience is running errands and fighting the red tape, or should it be the "Red" tape?

I managed to squeeze in a phone call to my folks in Rome from the post office. Everything was fine and they would try to plan a visit next month.

In the evening Marta came over once again, she was a really strong-willed lady I had to admit! Andrew and I tried to be polite though we were getting a bit fed up of her excessive and unwanted attention. She was so admirably determined we briefly half-seriously debated whether we should reward her persistence by granting her access to our beds (or one of them at least) for a limited time, but in the end we decided against it!

25 March 1980 – Jesus, *Chateaubriand* and Grignolino

In the morning we went to meet our economics professor in the faculty lounge of SGPiS and were treated to some *ciastko*, some delicious Polish pastry. Between classes today we ran into a lady called Larissa, the only Polish graduate of our very own Georgetown University's School of Foreign Service, whom we would meet again during our stay.

We also met Jesus, a black Cuban who was also studying at SGPiS as part of an exchange program among brother socialist countries. He invited us to visit his room in Madalinskiego for a drink of Cuban rum. I thought it was funny that in strictly and rigidly communist, yet deeply catholic, Cuba they still called young boys "Jesus".

In a way Poland and Cuba had this in common: a one-party system and state-run socialist economy installed a few decades eralier but a deep-rooted catholic culture dating back centuries. A far longer tradition than what marxism had been able to accumulate so far, or that it was ever likely to. I did not know about Cuba, I had never been there, but here most Poles we spoke with did not have a problem with that. Jesus Christ, in a way, was a socialist, speaking for the rights of the oppressed. Both Christ and Marx pointed to a better future. Although Marx concentrated more on this life and Christ on the next one, the communist utopia was so far in the future, especially if you lived in Poland in 1980, that most people would probably get to see perfect happiness in heaven first.

In the afternoon we had to run down to the Post Office on Jasna Swietokrzyska and place a call to Cathy and tell her to get a passport as she, like most Americans, had never had one before. As usual, they couldn't honor Ann's time slot reservation, everything was behind schedule. Cathy sounded amused when Ann finally got through.

By the end of the afternoon Ann and I decided to treat ourselves to another dinner at the always classy *Canaletto* restaurant, in the Victoria Hotel. We finally got to try their famed *Chateaubriand* steak and an easy young red Italian wine, Grignolino d'Asti from Italy's northwestern region of Piedmont. Excellent though not as exotic or exciting as bear or bison. With dessert, it came to 500 złoty per person. About five dollars. So cheap, for us.

26 March 1980 – East German plans and Cuban coffee

In the morning we drove to the East German embassy to pick up our visas. We had to pay six dollars per person for a double transit visa: thus equipped we would be able to travel into the DDR (*Deutsche Demokratische Republik*, German Democratic Republic) from Poland and out to West Berlin, then return the same way.

In the afternoon we were invited by two Cuban students, friends of Jesus, to have some coffee in their room. In addition to rum Cuba made excellent coffee of course and they claimed to have some of the best. Well, it was OK but not great, but then again I am Italian and always a bit finicky about my coffees.

Of course, most importantly, we appreciated the offer because it was interesting to meet new classmates (I realized they were the first Cubans I ever met, excluding some expats from Florida who attended Georgetown) and their coffee was in any case better than what was available in Poland.

In the evening I went with Christopher to another piano concert at the Chopin academy. It was a real pleasure to share my passion for classical music with him, though he was a somewhat mysterious character. He did not speak much about himself. He did not speak much at all in fact. He might have been a political agent charged with monitoring me for all I knew, but I did not care.

He told me that he knew two lady friends in East Berlin, and would have liked to introduce them to us. He was sure they would be delighted to have contacts with Italians and Americans but he said he feared for their safety should they be seen hanging around with nonauthorized western company. I told him I would be absolutely delighted to meet East German ladies and promised to be circumspect as the case may require. In the end he said it was better not to take any chances. The security police in East Germany, the notorious *Staatssicherheit* (state security) or Stasi, was known for molesting its own citizens at the least offense against communist discipline. Suspicion was often enough to prove guilt. And an unauthorized meeting with capitalist students could well be such an offense. Pity.

In the evening we had a few drinks with schoolmates in our room. We met Romek, a friend of Stefan's. He was a cool guy who spoke good Russian, French and German and some English. He said he taught himself English because that was the language he would need in the future. He had some experience abroad, having worked in the USSR and France. Very confident, he felt the system in Poland was a real straightjacket to opportunity and growth. He was a no-nonsense pragmatist, and had no confidence that the current system could ever be fixed, so he would want to have it changed completely, and as soon as possible.

In a short period of time, we became good friends with Romek, and learned a lot from his spontaneous yet always well informed off-the-cuff remarks on economics, politics, morals, and pretty much everything that had to do with Poland.

27 March 1980 – Socialist ideology and Cold War

Our usual morning class in socialist economics was hard to stay awake to. This particular professor was rather shy, and stuck very closely to the party line. He was more of a theoretical economist than a practical analyst of the "real socialism" we had come to experience. He talked to us more about Marx and Engels than of Lenin and Stalin. He steered wide clear of contemporary Polish and Soviet communist leaders such as Brezhnev, Gomułka and Gierek. In other words, he preferred theory to history and avoided politics. He clearly measured his words in order not to provoke controversy.

Of course, socialism in theory sounded beautiful to us, but in practice, human nature being what it is, much less so. No amount of altruism could do away with our innate sense of self-interest, no matter how much the latter could (and should) be moderated by a vision for the common good, by moral considerations and ultimately, fundamentally, by the rule of law.

Even though I was really interested in trying to find out how socialist theories imagined to do away with the inescapable economic laws of demand and supply, this guy was just plain boring.

Afterwards we drove to the central railway station where we tried, and failed, to buy our train tickets to East Berlin. The reason was that we needed to bring our passports, our DDR visas (which we had not yet received) and the receipt for our official money exchange. We would have to come back another day. I was annoyed and frustrated, could not believe they required all this paperwork just to sell a train ticket to a "brother" socialist country.

In the afternoon we had four hours of foreign policy classes at the Center for International Studies. As usual it was all quite official and bureaucratic. However I got the definite impression that some of the professors spoke to the limit of what was considered politically acceptable. I was sure they would have said more if they had felt safe doing so. They were card carrying Communists, or at least pretended to be, but they were clearly first of all Poles, and that usually took priority.

Maybe it would have been more interesting to meet them over a glass of vodka rather than in the classroom, but that was too difficult to organize given our position as students about to receive grades from the profs. Looking back, we should have at least tried.

Today's cherry on the pie was a discussion on why the U.S. dropped the bomb on Hiroshima. Our professor insisted that the real purpose was not so much to defeat Japan but to demonstrate its might to the USSR and that THAT was the beginning of the cold war. It was America's fault. It was America's fault, not the Soviet Union's for blockading Berlin or forcing single-party communism down the throat of neighboring countries. Nonetheless he most likely did a point about the president Truman's desire to flex muscles to Stalin's face.

We picked up a bite to eat in the Forum: Ann ice cream and Andrew venison. Poland offers really good game if you can find it. I went for bigoš, also known as hunter's stew, a Polish specialty that consists of finely chopped mixed meats stewed together with sauerkraut shredded cabbage. Not exactly a light dish but so tasty and so Polish!

In the evening there was a party in Zbyszek's room. Nine men and two women, so it was not so interesting after all. A girl called Marzena was there though and she looked quite pretty and would quickly prove to be the most friendly and open Polish girl we had met so far. She was a friend of Larissa's and apparently knew very well a certain Tony, the American who attended our exchange program at SGPiS the previous year.

28 March 1980 – Socialist ping pong

After our usual classes we went for lunch at the *Staropolska* (old Poland) restaurant. Good if basic meal. Then three more hours of foreign policy classes at the Center for International Affairs.

Later on we went to fill up the tank at our usual gas station, where by now we had become friends with all the staff and proceeded with our usual "Polish" price purchase. It had become so routine, compared to the first few weeks when everyone was so much more circumspect! It really honestly did not feel we were doing anything wrong. Illegal yes but not wrong, we felt.

In the evening we were joined by a group of Polish, Vietnamese and Mongol (both countries were "socialist brothers" of Poland) students for an international ping pong tournament at the student house. We won some and lost some.

Too bad the Chinese were not there, they were the best at this game and it would have been fun to share a night with them, not just for the ping pong. But unfortunately the Chinese Communist Party has long broken ranks with the Soviets and their east European satellites. The Mongols and the Vietnamese, on the other hand, were best friends with the Soviet Union, in part because of their shared mistrust and fear of China. Both countries were associated with the Council for Mutual Economic Assistance (aka Comecon) as was Cuba, the only three non European members.

Mongolia was sometimes referred to as "Outer Mongolia" by China, as opposed to the adjacent "Inner Mongolia" which was already a Chinese province. The "outer" Mongols did not want to join their "inner" brethren inside China. The latter might not want to stay there either but did not have a choice. When Mongolia became an independent state in the 1920s it was in large part thanks to Soviet assistance. The Chinese considered the Mongols to be Chinese, really:

after all the great Chinese emperors Genghis Khan and Kublai Khan, and their Yuan dynasty that ruled China for a century and we learned about from Marco Polo, were Mongols.

Therefore the government in Ulaan Bataar, the capital of Mongolia, had always been aligned with Moscow, whether Imperial Tsarist Russia or Communist USSR. I was sure if one day the USSR were to become capitalist, Mongolia would immediately discover the benefits of profit and private property! Anything to keep out the Chinese, even send ping pong playing students to Warsaw! China, truth be told, does not officially claim any territory from Mongolia.

Vietnam had long had a difficult relationship with China, since well before both countries became communist. During the war against the French and the Americans the Soviets helped a lot and after the Sino-Soviet split China feared a continued Soviet presence on its southern border. So China helped a friendly Communist Party, the genocidal *Khmer Rouge*, take power in neighboring Cambodia. Vietnam invaded and kicked them out of power. Last year China briefly invaded Vietnam to "punish" it. After a few weeks both sides claimed victory and the Chinese troops went home. The Vietnamese army stayed put in the Cambodian capital Phnom Penh, China grabbed a little bit of border land from Vietnam and some 60,000 people died in battle.

All of this made me think about "socialist brother countries" who fought each other, not just in ideological Cold Wars but real, hot wars in the battlefield. Of course, each side purported to represent the real socialism, while accusing the other of betraying the original ideals of Marx, Engels and Lenin. (No one gave Stalin much credit any more, at least not openly, and Mao was clearly only for China to adore and even there he was losing his shine very fast since Deng came to power.)

29 March 1980 – A song for the Polish pope

At 2:30 in the afternoon we drove to meet Jasmina, a friend of some Americans of Polish descent who lived in Pascoag, Andrew's home village in the state of Rhode Island. Andrew had been put in touch with her and she invited us to the house where she lived with her sister, a bit outside of Warsaw. It took us a little while to find it in an unfamiliar neighborhood. The word "house" might have been an overstatement: it consisted of one room, without any bathroom, no running water, and a wood-burning stove for heating.

Very welcoming, she and her sister deployed a predictable array of drinks and food, though it was not meal time. Of course we had to eat and drink all of it. Very simple people, they gave us all they could and were excited to meet us, unlikely they would meet many foreigners very often. She said she made 5,000 złoty per month, about the national average in those days.

After we had eaten and drunk, Jasmina pulled out a cassette player and started playing some Italian songs about pope John Paul II by I am not sure which singer. She asked me to translate them. The only way that could work was for me to translate into English and Ann then would translate from English into Polish. JP II was clearly a superstar here, and his visit last year was, by far, the most memorable event to have taken place in the country in many decades. We made their day!

I spent the evening out with Marzena, we walked around looking for a place to have a drink but somehow all bars were full on this Saturday night. Poles could not really splurge but knew how to have fun! Dinner at the hotel *Victoria*, good food and a good deal as usual. Pleasant conversation with Marzena, who was open minded and very talkative about her (mostly negative) experience in making ends meet in Warsaw. She seemed to have no secrets of any kind, and was eager to share it all, even if I avoided asking too many questions. Somehow I did not feel as comfortable asking her questions about Poland as I did with my university classmates. Not sure why. Interesting person.

After dinner, when we walked back to the car that I had parked on a nearby street, we found a policeman waiting for us. He wanted to give me a fine for illegal parking. I did not think I had parked illegally in all honesty but that was besides the point. He looked very serious and threatened to notify the Italian embassy if I didn't pay. Maybe he wanted a bribe, or maybe he liked Marzena, but I was not sure what to do. I did not think the Italian embassy would or should care about such a trifling episode in the life of an Italian citizen.

I was tempted to call his bluff and almost told him to please go ahead and notify the Italian embassy, I was sure they would be sooo interested in this grave matter in bilateral Polish-Italian relations that they would devote their utmost attention to it. I could see the frown on the face of the ambassador when he was notified I had refused to pay for a parking ticket!

Marzena finally managed to talk him into letting us go. With Marzena's help, I simply told him I had no money, though what I really meant was I had to money to waste on a bogus fine especially as it was likely he would just keep the cash for himself. He thought about it for a few seconds and then turned around and left us alone. That was easier than expected, Marzena's persuasive powers were astonishing!

30 March 1980 – News about Katyn

Easy Sunday, or at least it started easy. We got together with a few friends in our room for a late breakfast of *kanapki* and vodka. Not the usual breakfast I grew up with, but we were eager to give it a try.

Ann, Romek, Tadek and one of the ping pong players we met a few days ago whose name I missed all joined Andrew and me for a bite and a few glasses of the transparent Polish "water of life". Initially it felt a bit weird to eat sausage and cucumber on top of open sandwiches first thing in the morning, and even more so to drink vodka, but then we developed a taste for it and well, we were in Poland after all, so we took it as a cultural experience. And in fact we liked it quite a bit, and no need fur lunch after a late breakfast of this kind.

Our Polish friends conveyed some harrowing news: a man in his seventies set himself on fire at the Krakow memorial to the victims of Katyn. Katyn, we all knew, was a forest in western Russia, near Smolensk, where in 1940 the Soviet secret police carried out one of the most heinous crimes of World War II.

As it happened, when Germany invaded Poland in 1939, thousands of Polish officers fled to the USSR thinking they would be safe and could organize themselves to resume the fight for their homeland. Wrong.

Hitler and Stalin had agreed an infamous secret protocol to the 1939 Molotov-Ribbentrop Nonaggression Pact whereby they would carve up Poland between them and erase it from the map as an independent country. Not the first time this happened: already in the XVIII century Russia, Prussia, and Austria-Hungary had partitioned

Poland, and it had regained independence only after World War I, barely twenty years before being invaded again.

Instead of getting help to fight what they thought was a common cause against the Nazis, the Polish officers were shot, together with scores of land owners, intellectuals, priests, and other undesirables, about 22,000 of them all in all. They were buried in large pits at Katyn.

When, in 1941, Germany decided that the 1939 Pact no longer served its purposes and invaded the USSR, they found the bodies. The Soviets accused the Germans of the killings. The Germans denied responsibility and called the Red Cross to inspect the mass graves. It might be strange to imagine the SS cooperating with the Red Cross, but they did, because it obviously served Nazi propaganda well to do so.

The Red Cross, after detailed forensic examinations, dutifully announced that the killings had taken place well before Germany invaded, which put the blame squarely on the Soviets. The shame for the USSR was formidable, but Stalin and his successors simply denied the facts and continued to accuse Germany of having killed the Poles. The Americans and the British needed the Soviet Union to fight the Axis more than they needed to seek justice for Poland and did not pursue the matter.

That lie still officially stood in 1980, at least in Poland and in the other socialist countries of eastern Europe. The rest of the world knew better.

Apparently the poor man in Krakow who killed himself today was one of the few of the Polish officers who had made it out alive at Katyn in 1940. Today's Polish newspapers did not mention anything about what happened but the ping pong player had a brother who lived in Krakow and he had told him over the phone.

The subject of the Katyn massacre was pretty much off limits in Poland. Everyone knew the politically incorrect truth (the Soviets did it) but no one was allowed to say, let alone print, anything other than the ridiculous propaganda line (the Germans did it) and so most Poles preferred to just ignore the issue. The poor man who set himself on fire was probably sick of this fiction and lack of respect for the fellow countrymen who died such a cruel and (unless you were Stalin) useless death in 1940.

We were all in a somber mood after the news.

Tadek told us about his brother's studies at the military academy. Apparently they had to study American weapons (know your enemy!) and the best instructors were Vietnamese soldiers who had recent first hand experience with the stuff!

31 March 1980 – Ice skating and drinks

Usual morning classes and homework in the dorm in the afternoon. At 6:30pm Andrew, Ann and I met Marzena at school and went for a skating session at a nearby ice rink. Marzena was quite good at it, and so was Andrew. Ann could put on a respectable show but I was just pathetic. Anyway it was fun.

Later out for a drink at the *Krokodyl* restaurant where we made the acquaintance of Rani, a young Indian who worked in Tehran for an Italian company. Interesting guy. It was a difficult moment between the Americans and the Iranians: after the fall of the Shah the revolutionary Islamic government had taken a strong anti-western, and especially anti-American, line in foreign policy. A few months ago a large group of students had stormed the American embassy and taken everyone hostage. Dozens of people locked up in the building with no access to the outside world. But for him it was business as usual. I forgot to ask him why he was in Poland.

As I prepared for sleep I thought it was hard to believe March was already over, we were moving ahead with our course and our exciting experiences in Poland. Our adventure was almost half-way through and actually I sort of began to feel at home here. I had learnt enough Polish to carry on a basic conversation, order duck (and a few other things) at restaurants, buy ice cream and break ice with the locals. All in all it was way beyond my expectations when I decided to sign up last autumn.

1 April 1980 – Train tickets to the DDR and Russian caviar

After class Andrew, Ann and I spent about five hours in various travel offices trying, unsuccessfully, to buy our train tickets to East Berlin. We even changed some money legally, at the official exchange rate (it was the second time since we arrived in Poland, the first being on our very first day just past the border, and we knew it would probably be the last) to demonstrate the legal provenance for our currency. It really felt weird to change money officially, in a bank. Shame on us!

But then some ticket-issuing authority clerk told us we had the wrong receipt. They had never mentioned that there was more than one kind of receipt for foreign currency exchange. And they were serious, despite today's date it was no April Fool's joke. Or maybe they were not serious serious, they just wanted a bribe. We did not think of that possibility then. A few dollars under the counter might have solved the problem for us and made everyone happy.

We would have to wait and see, but it seemed this short trip to East Germany was rapidly becoming more trouble than it was ever going to be worth.

At 7:00 in the evening Marta came to visit in my room. I was alone, Andrew was out, which worried me considerably. In her unceasing efforts to win my favors she had actually made a huge Polish flag for me. I collected flags from the countries I visited and some days back I had mentioned to her I would have liked a Polish flag to take home. A Polish flag was easy to make, just two large white and red bands stitched together. She had made a huge one with a silky golden ribbon on all sides.

Luckily we were soon joined by Marzena and Andrew, who had gone out for a walk in town. After a while I thanked Marta for the flag but gracefully let her go home, then took Marzena out for dinner to the *Staropolska* restaurant.

Here I tried black caviar, real Russian caviar, for the first time in my life. It tasted really good, a new and surprising flavor and an unusual consistency, but I liked it. It was the Beluga kind, the rarest and most expensive, roe from huge sturgeon fish in the Caspian sea. It was served on soft white small bread buns called *blini* in I am not sure what language, with some butter. And of course plenty of vodka.

Caviar was readily available in Poland – if you had hard currency, that is. Much of it was smuggled in from the USSR where it was produced by the Caspian sea. Because it was highly sought by western tourists, diplomats, dollar-making middle class, anyone who could afford it really, its exportation to the West was strictly regulated. It could be taken out of Poland only if one could demonstrate that it had been bought legally, at artificially inflated prices, and virtually no one did. Everyone except, perhaps, the most visible restaurants, bought the stuff in the informal farmers markets from the smugglers.

During the course of my stay in Poland I would have quite a few chances to buy it at various markets. Usually the price was fifty American dollars for a 2kg can that was worth several thousand dollars in the West but had been paid peanuts in the USSR, where supply was not regulated by market prices but by privileged access to the producers.

Marzena was a fine lady and even though we were just friends, and I had no plans to change that, I decided to invite her to visit me in Italy at the end of our semester. At first, she did not believe me, or at least pretended not to believe me. Also, she was not sure how to put this to her parents, they might not have liked her traveling abroad with a man she was not married to, nor planning to marry. So we agreed that probably the best way was for her to be invited to the United States by Ann, or at least to tell that to her parents.

A personal official invitation was indispensable for a Polish citizen to get a visa from most western countries and it also makes it easier to get a passport from the government of Poland. That was because western governments wanted to be sure the invitee did not become a financial burden in case of trouble, and the Polish government did not want to incur any costs should anything happen to one of its citizens while the visit was taking place. Of course, Ann could invite her to the States while I could invite her to Italy.

We westerners from liberal democracies talked a lot about freedom of travel, and criticized the socialist countries for not letting their people out easily. But it occurred to me it was easier for a Pole to exit Poland than to enter a western country.

2 April 1980 – Shopping and more study

Some more shopping for clothes in town, I needed a smart casual jacket and new trousers to go to some theater events. Ann and I went around for a while and finally stumbled in a nondescript department store, mostly empty and otherwise stocked with very poor quality stuff. Finally I bought an almost decent kaki colored suit for 2,250 złoty. I was never difficult when it comes to clothes, in fact I never really cared, but this was really at the borderline of my acceptance threshold. The cloth was rough, but it was the best there was, anywhere in the city.

After which we went to the post office to call Cathy, Ann's friend in Washington who planned to join us for a tour of Europe at the end of our course. Ann mentioned to her for the first time that we would have liked to drive to the Soviet Union, and while it was not the typical European tour of her dreams, she was not opposed to the idea. Ann had feared she would be reluctant as she had little travel experience. The USSR was a large black hole in the mind of most people on our side of the iron curtain, it inspired curiosity in some but diffidence, if not fear, in most.

She initially had said she wanted to see all of Europe in a few weeks, because she was not sure she would ever come back. Apparently that was the way many Americans saw a trip to Europe: a bit like a trip to the moon. I always noticed groups of Japanese tourists in Rome shooting pictures of everything as if it was the last thing they would ever see in their life. Rather gloomy prospect.

But Ann talked to her and explained that it was much better to see less but understand more, go deeper. As I thought about it, I was really lucky to have Ann and Andrew as my travel companions, we shared a strong motivation to understand, which required time and attention to detail. Never hurry. This trip would not have been nearly as fun and instructive without them.

End of the day spent studying in the apartment I had rented for my parents, I managed to get the keys from the landlord a couple of weeks before their arrival and enjoyed the privacy away from the dorm. I guess I paid too much for the rent so he was quite willing to let me use it for three times as long as the planned duration of my folks' stay. More cheap and cheerful pasta and red wine for dinner. I knew I had better take advantage of it while it lasted.

3 April 1980 – Train tickets and church music

After the usual morning classes I went to get my hair cut at a barber shop in the Forum Hotel. Ninety-two złotys, shampoo included, pretty cheap and a good job.

Then Romek accompanied the three of us to buy our train tickets to Berlin. Despite the thorough preparatory work of the previous days, we needed his help to overcome the indefatigable

Polish bureaucracy. At one point a clerk wanted us to change money again, because the receipt of the money we changed yesterday had a different date (yesterday) than the date on the receipt of the train tickets (today). We managed to stay cool and Romek persuaded the man to finally issue our tickets.

In the evening we went for a concert of Luke's passion by Johann Sebastian Bach in a small protestant church in downtown. Always a moving experience to listen to Bach's religious music, even if I am not religious. The pews of the Holy Trinity Lutheran church were very uncomfortable, maybe to ensure the faithful would suffer for their sins. This church was significant because for centuries no protestant churches were allowed to be built Poland. You had to be catholic or you were out of luck. This building changed things at the end of the XVIII century. Chopin played here during the first half of the XIX and after its post World War II reconstruction it continued to be a leading musical venue.

4 April 1980 - Bureaucracy and a concert

After classes and normal errands (standing in lines, filling out forms) we decided to take advantage of the fact that Ann's room was free as her roommates had gone home for Easter. We bought wine, cheese, bread and *pasztet* (a kind of cake). We had to stand in several lines at various shops to collect all we needed but at the end we could have a party in Ann's room. At 3:00 in the afternoon they began to broadcast Jesus Christ Superstar. We relaxed and listened.

In the evening Ann and I went to the *Sala Koncertowa* to hear a harpsichord program: not exactly my favorite instrument, especially for a whole concert, but we had nothing better to do really as lots of places were shut for the holidays and many friends had gone home.

5 April 1980 – Częstochowa

Today we needed to fill up Giallina but our gas station was closed so we tried another one. They didn't know us so we had to be a bit circumspect in negotiating a price. They readily agreed to sell for 28 złoty per liter. This was much more than the 18 złoty we usually paid at our friends' station but still much less than the official 75 złoty we were supposed to pay as foreigners using the official coupons.

Easy and pleasant trip to Częstochowa. The further south we went, the more snow we encountered, although it did not amount to more than maybe some 10 centimeters by the road side. It was not a problem for driving.

Instead of taking the popular, well traveled roads, we chose to wander along some country roads through such places as Bółchatów and Sulmierzyce and Bogomicowce, where Ann and I went to explore a little country church. Much to our surprise, in it we discovered a set up of the "Tomb of Christ" complete with a Christ statue, candles, and two men dressed in medieval garb, complete with visor and alabard, standing guard.

In Sulmierzyce, the local parish priest was excited to see our car plate from Rome, straight from the city of the Polish pope, and insisted to take us into the church and introduce us to the parishioners. Many people were there for the Easter blessing. Before he performed the traditional blessing of the baskets, he introduced us to his parishioners and they all, smiling and nodding, turned around and wished us a heartfelt Happy Easter. Afterwards, he presented each of us with a *pisanka,* a special Polish Easter egg, and then gave us a tour of his beautiful church, pointing out to us the items laid out in preparation for tomorrow's sunrise procession. He was especially proud of the intricately embroidered Easter banners.

Interesting to note that in this church, and others in small villages, a statue of Christ is guarded by two statues of medieval soldiers. I was not able to get a good explanation as of why the soldiers were necessary, I would have to research it a bit more.

We kept driving along and run into a Soviet military cemetery. No crosses of course, just red stars and plain stones on the graves. The grass was rough and uneven, the whole place emanated an air of neglect.

The Soviets were not loved in Poland, to put it mildly, but the official party line was that they liberated the country from the Nazi invasion. Which was true, except that they had partitioned the same country in together with the Nazi in 1939, and except also that they did not really "liberate" it, as in give it freedom, but rather subjected it to a new dictatorship.

When we finally arrived in Częstochowa it was really cold, there was a lot of snow on the ground. You would not think this was April!

After some effort we located our hotel, the Orbis-Patria,[13] at the foot of the mountain to Jasna Góra. However they only had one twin room left and the three of us had to squeeze into two beds, there was no choice. We were lucky to get even that, it was Easter after all and we were in the most sacred location of the whole country.

After we left our stuff in the room we walked to the monastery through the mist and snow. The cathedral looked awesome in a way that none of the churches in Warsaw ever could. Maybe because it was actually the original building, it had not been destroyed by wars and that gave it an ineffable charm. Once inside, behind an iron gate, was the historic picture of the "Black Madonna", a Byzantine icon that had been the most venerated holy image of Poland for over half a millennium.

Again, we were amazed by the tasteful, if richly ornate, clusters of jewels around the somber portrait. Maybe we were more in awe of the spiritual significance of the painting than of either its pictorial features or its technical achievement, but we stood there speechless for a little while. We were fortunate to have come at Easter for the portrait is rarely exhibited.

We explored the monastery still further and somewhere wandered into the organ loft from where we were able to get full view of the proceedings below. The organ master was a friendly man and asked Ann if she was interested in music. He became more animated when he discovered we were foreigners and gladly tried out his Italian on me. He had been the organist of the monastery for 13 years and his eyes lit up recalling the Pope's visit last May. He was enthusiastically insistent that we remain in the organ loft another hour for a choir was coming which would sing Handel's *Halleluja*. However, we had not eaten anything all day and preferred to feed our bodies and not our spirits. In retrospect I regretted that decision.

We took a forgettable bite to eat in the hotel before retiring into our twin bed room. Who shared a bed with whom shall remain a secret!

6 April 1980 – Easter day procession in Jasna Gora

We decided to brave the weather and got up very early in the morning to go and witness the Easter procession. In this very holy

---

[13] *This later became the Hotel Mercure Częstochowa Centrum.*

town it had been recommended to us as an event not to be missed. We were out of the hotel at the crack of dawn, by 5:30am or so. It was VERY cold! We wanted to make it to the Basilica before 6 in the morning so as not to miss the Easter Procession complete with banners and fanfare. At the time we didn't understand why a mass was already being celebrated even though we arrived before 6. There probably had been no procession outside of the Basilica since the ground was pure icy slush.

A full orchestra and choir again performed, and this time for us, Handel's *Halleluja*. We explored the slushy ramparts, making the way of the cross, until my boots could hold out no more of the dampness.

Afterwards we were quite tired so Ann and I took a nap while Andrew hung out at the Basilica. It was here that we realized why we had missed the beginning of the ceremony: Poland had switched to daylight saving time, our watches were late!

The Jasna Gora monastery was imposing, surely the most impressive site we had seen so far in Poland. It was the heart of Christianity in the country. Here, almost a year ago, Pope John Paul II delivered his farewell speech at the end of a trip that stirred religious as well as political emotions in Catholic Poland.

At the Black Madonna there was a considerable number of people praying and kneeling. The atmosphere was charged with spiritual energy.

The multiple processions at the Jasna Gora monastery started at six o'clock, but they were not as impressive as we expected. Not so many people after all. Hundreds, not thousands, despite the fact that is was Easter day. How come all the hotel rooms were booked solid? Maybe there were not that many rooms to begin with.

Rather frugal Easter arrangements, maybe resources were limited. Surely they had to be. Yet we expected to find a lot more people and enthusiasm in the wake of the Polish Pope's recent galvanizing visit.

Ann drove Giallina for most of the way home in an attempt to perfect her mastery of the manual stick shift. She did pretty well. We arrived in Warsaw around 9 and went to the hotel *Europejski* to have our Easter dinner.

7 April 1980 – Getting ready for East Germany

Afternoon spent packing for Berlin. We would not be driving our trusted Giallina this time so we needed to prepare essential stuff to carry with us. We thought about driving but we decided against it because we did not have so much time for this trip. Also, the last thing we wanted, should anything happen, was to get in any sort of trouble with the notorious East German police in the middle of our academic semester. And finally, we wanted to visit West Berlin as well, which would mean another two crossings of the iron curtain in its most dreadful incarnation: the Berlin Wall. So it was going to be a night train. Easier through the borders and more efficient use of our limited time.

We also decided not to spend any night in East Berlin hotels. We could have, but the bureaucratic complications involved in making the mandatory advance reservations put us off. So we decided to travel at night, reach East Berlin early in the morning, spend a whole day there then cross over to West Berlin and visit this bastion of capitalist democracy in the middle of a communist ocean for a day or two before traveling in the opposite direction, spend another part of a day in East Berlin and again hop on a night train back to Poland.

Another advantage of this plan was that we would have easy access to normal West German shops and could stock up with essentials like good toothpaste, film for our cameras, batteries... Oh, and good chocolate, one of the few things we actually really missed in Poland!

8 April 1980 – Departure to Berlin

After our classes and some last minute packing, in the late afternoon we boarded our long-desired train for East Berlin. It had taken us so long to get the tickets, visas and legal cash we had almost given up. But now we were on.

The spring days were getting longer and before it became completely dark we got a glimpse of the flatlands of western Poland, the so long fought-over Pomerania. German land for centuries, it had been given to Poland after World War II, both to punish the Nazi and to compensate Poland for the land it had to surrender to the Soviet Union and Soviet-occupied Lithuania.

The train was fairly comfortable, though we did not have tickets for a sleeper car. So we made do with regular seats, though we did buy tickets for the "soft" part of the train, where seats had cushions and were actually quite comfortable, at least to sit on. Not easy to spend a whole night on while trying to catch some sleep but we did it.

Romek, who was flat-out in partying mode, invited us to drink and make merry in his compartment, where he, his brother and his friend Zbyszek had ample supplies of vodka for the purpose. We shared a few shots and then went back to our compartment.

We finally fell asleep, sort of, knowing it was going to be a fascinating experience but a little worried about visiting a country ruled by a communist party with a reputation for being much stricter and less forgiving than that of Poland.

9 April 1980 – A taste of East and on to the West Berlin

At the ungodly hour of 4 or 5 in the morning we crossed the Polish German border. Neither the Polish border guards nor the Germans were kind enough to let us sleep through the brotherly line! First the Poles woke us up to check our passports and then the East Germans did the same a few minutes later. All went smoothly and we collapsed back into our seats for another couple of hours.

At 7 am we arrived at a cold, rainy East Berlin. It was too early for anything to open yet so we stopped in a cafe off Alexanderplatz. The dollar-East Mark official exchange rate was so outrageously incongruous that we had to bum 20 marks off Zbyszek, who had changed money who knows where, or we would have simply thrown our money out the window. We did not know how to change money in the local black market, and we did not want to know, it was not worth the risk.

We walked out of the station and were in the heart of the DDR, the *Deutsche Demokratische Republik*, aka the German Democratic Republic. This country was German, yes, we knew how better disciplined and predictable, even stultified, this Soviet satellite was compared to Poland.

Republic, OK yes, the DDR was not a monarchy, though you could say the secretive and omnipotent Socialist Unity Party of Germany (*Sozialistische Einheitspartei Deutschlands*, or SED, the long-winded name for the local communist party) was a kind of oligarchy. The name itself was rather Orwellian: whatever you thought of the party, no one in his right mind could believe it was really working for German unity. A divided Germany was the *raison d'être* of the SED; German re-unification would almost surely make it redundant.

Democratic the DDR was certainly not, in whichever direction you could stretch the meaning of the word.

It occurred to me that any country that called itself "democratic", wasn't! And no country that really could be classified as "democratic" by any reasonable yardstick bothered to call itself such. But of course, in communist ideology, to be "democratic" (etymologically: power of the people) was seen as a source of legitimation. Anything the party did was for the people. Including suppressing the people when they did not understand what was in their own best interest.

The city center was clean and every corner was almost manicured. First things first, we climbed on top of the *Fernsehturm*, the TV tower that is a point of reference for anyone moving around East Berlin. Built between 1965 and 1969 it was the tallest structure in all of Germany[14] and a symbol of pride for the authorities of the DDR. Unfortunately because of the weather we could not see much from the top: it no longer rained but we could see just clouds and fog, pity.

As we walked around over the next few hours we discovered that not all parts of the city were as spotless as we thought after our first impression around the station: many streets were dirty, buildings were neglected and wall plaster was cracked, they qualified for the title of slums really.

A few churches were available in this most strict Communist dictatorship. Re-built after the war, they were mostly empty shells of bricks and concrete. No decorations. Only a few pieces of low-relief sculptures were on display, recuperated from the pre-war works. The DDR even had a so-called Christian Democracy political party, but it was completely subservient to the SED, however. Not even close to their equivalent in the Federal Republic (aka as West Germany), the

---

14 *Note in 2018: it still is!*

party of Adenauer which pulled West Germany up from the ruins of the war.

We then visited the Palace of Culture and the History Museum, both places were replete with vicious attacks against the West in every shape or form: paintings, posters, caricatures. The West was full of thieves, exploiters of the workers, smugglers, warmongers. It was almost comical were it not for the fact that it was very sad to think this was all that was allowed in a major state institution like this museum.

It was getting late in the day and we moved slowly toward the border. Funny to think of a border in the middle of a city. But when the victorious powers of World War II divided Germany up into four occupation zones to prevent its resurgence as a threat to peace, they could not agree on who would hold Berlin, which was smack inside the Soviet zone. So they decided to cut it up four ways too. (France managed to persuade the others that it, too, had won the war, though in fact it surrendered after three weeks of fighting and Vichy France helped Nazi Germany more than Fascit Italy ever did. But this is another story.)

The problem, for the Soviets, was that unhappy East Germans kept walking over to the American, French or British sectors to escape the socialist dictatorship they had set up in theirs. After a few years this exodus was bleeding East Germany of its best people, and Erich Honecker, a communist apparatchik who was now the country's leader, came up with the idea of building a wall around the three western sectors so as to physically prevent citizens trapped into the Soviet sector from getting access to them. It was built virtually overnight in 1961 and then repeatedly reinforced and equipped with surveillance equipment. Guards were placed along the wall and over 200 people lost their lives trying to jump over, mostly shot dead by East German sharpshooters.

By the end of the day we tried to walk across the wall at the famous Brandenburg gate but before we could even get anywhere close to it we understood that was a no go. Strictly off limits. No one had walked under the arches of the gate for years.

We then tried to walk into West Berlin through check-point *Charlie*, which was a functioning transit point, but for some reason we were not allowed to do so. We tried to ask but could never understand why. Maybe there was no "why". We could only travel to

West Berlin by metro, crossing at the Friedrichstrasse station. This was a unique station because it was in East Berlin but it was served by West Berlin metro, so it became a border station, allowing for a more easily controlled border crossing.

The old pre-war German metro was still functioning but of course it, too, was divided in half. However, its underground tunnels had obviously not been planned with Allied and Soviet occupation in mind! Some stations had to be closed, literally walled up, as the trains travelled under East Berlin to go from one part of West Berlin to another. Other stations in West Berlin were closed, too, to prevent some East German to jump onto the platform and fall into the capitalist pit. It was kind of funny in a macabre sort of way to imagine that we were on one side one minute, and beyond the wall the next, then back again. We could decide where to spend the night, of course, but the East Germans could not.

In fact this experience made me think of the wall. Not only the physical wall that scars the city of Berlin, but the political, economic, and most importantly social and psychological wall that cut Europe in half. I had grown up and studied at school that the Communists lived on the other side of the wall. The wall separated them from us.

But scarcely two months in Poland, mixing and mingling with Polish colleagues, I no longer felt on the other side of the wall. I sympathized with our oppressed friends under Communist rule and felt that it was my country Italy, West Germany with glittering West Berlin, that were beyond the wall. The United States, where I went to university, my second home, was so much beyond the wall you could hardly imagine how far it was. For most Poles, let alone East Germans, it might as well have been on another planet.

When we emerged from the West Berlin metro station we started looking for a place to sleep, and enjoyed walking around the sparkling smart city for a few kilometers even though it was raining and we had to carry our bags. Very expensive for us after we had gotten used to Polish prices! But you could actually buy anything you wanted at clear, transparent prices. No black market, and we exchanged US dollars for west German D-marks in a real bank.

By evening we found a mediocre room with three beds in a bed and breakfast by the sinister name of "Buchenwald"[15] for 26 D-

---

15 *Buchenwald ("beech forest") was the name of one of the most notorious Nazi prisoners of war and internment camps, where over 50,000 people*

marks per day. We were very tired after a long day walking around and we had not really had a full night of sleep on the train, so we collapsed soon after 8 o'clock, and would sleep for a solid twelve hours.

10 April 1980 – Exploring West Berlin

Early in the morning we were unceremoniously ejected from our guesthouse with Teutonic precision not one minute later than the advertised check-out time of 10 o'clock. Which was just as good or we might have spent the whole day in bed. We then started looking for another place to spend the following night.

Through a tourist office we found a homestay: a couple of rooms for rent in the house of a friendly eighty-year-old woman in the district of Charlottenburg. It was a beautiful home, clearly upper-middle class, if not more, and looked grand despite being a bit tired, with its furniture and decorations that reminded us of what must have been a more glorious but distant past.

As soon as we arrived the landlady, Mrs. Born, a German who was born in Torun, a city that today is in Poland, and had lived some years in Gdansk when it was German and called Danzig, started a friendly conversation, partly in German and partly in her broken but gentle English. (She had totally forgotten her Polish so Ann was disappointed that she could not practice.) When she heard we were studying in Poland, she started telling us her stories about the war.

Over cakes and tea she told us she had lived in Gdansk (then Danzig) in the 1930s, and saw the first German ground attack *Stukas* aircraft dive bomb Poland on 1 September 1939, the first day of World War II.[16] She also said she saw German battleships shell Polish territory at Westerplatte but not a single shot coming in the other direction. She was not nostalgic of pre-war Germany, of course, but quite a bit worried about living in divided contemporary Germany, especially in isolated West Berlin. She felt World War II had not yet ended.

---

were killed.

16 *That is common wisdom at least in the West. If you talk to the Chinese they are likely to tell you that World War II really started in 1937 with the Japanese invasion of China, and they have a point.*

In the afternoon we visited Charlottenburg and the big radio tower. We walked for many kilometers, I was quite exhausted by the end of the day. We were impressed by the Kaiser Wilhelm Memorial Church, left the way it was after an Allied air raid in 1943, as a reminder of the horrors of war.

Dinner at a simple Italian restaurant, *San Giorgio*, OK quality and cheap, what we needed. Italian food abroad is rarely as good as at home in Italy, and if it is, it is too expensive, so I normally avoid it, but tonight it was OK, inexpensive and filling, excellent for three students on the go! Ann, perhaps wisely, opted for Belgian-style mussels and fries.[17]

We then walked around the city some more, aimlessly, hopping from one *Bierstube* (a German pub) to the next without any particular goal or target in mind. We walked past a few sex workers and drunks. After a few good cold blond German beers it was time to savor a good sleep, knowing there would be no early checkout tomorrow. Not before Andrew recited some poetry though! All of which was accompanied by a violin playing Paganini in the next apartment. German cakes, English poetry and Italian classical music made for a very pleasant end of the evening.

11 April 1980 – *Reichstag* and *Tiergarten*

Lazy wake up call at 9:30 and long walk in the *Tiergarten*, literally an "animals garden", a zoo, but in reality one of the largest urban parks in Europe. It was actually a balmy day with a blue sky, finally!!

We saw the Victory Column, enjoyed a great panoramic view from the top and walked all the way up to the Brandenburg Gate (the one we had fantasized of walking under), from which we could see

---

17   *Americans often refer to this typical side dish as "French fries": the habit apparently started during World War I when American soldiers were served the crispy potatoes by Belgian francophones behind the front lines and thought they were French. Who knows, they eat fries in northern France too, though* les frites *have long been a national dish in Belgium, you can find them at almost every corner of every street of every town. They are different from any other fried potatoes in that they are cooked in two successive phases in cow fat. They are one of the few things that truly unify Walloons and Flemish, the others being Trappist beer and the Red Devils, the national soccer team.*

the Berlin Wall and beyond it, East Berlin. Nearby we could also visit a colossal monument to the Soviet soldiers who conquered ("liberated", according to the Soviet terminology) Berlin. However, unsurprisingly, there were no West Berliners visiting the shrine, actually there was no one at all!

We also visited a history museum in the old *Reichstag* (parliament) building, kind of boring, not nearly as much fun as the one in the East! This building exuded history, it was here that the German Empire had its seat from 1894 and it was a fire in this building that helped newly appointed Chancellor Hitler to consolidate his grip on power in 1933. Now however it had a tired, beat-up look, unimpressive and underwhelming. It could use some major renovation but such an initiative was too politically sensitive to propose.

An interesting exhibit in the building was a collection of Deutsche Reichsmark notes from the 1920s, when Germany experienced hyperinflation and developed a sort of paranoia for expansionist monetary policies that will last many decades. One-billion-mark notes seemed small change. I was struck by a Reichsmark 200,000,000,000 (two-hundred-billion-mark) bank note! That looked like serious money!

Not far there was a platform on which we could climb via a short staircase. On top of the platform we could see East Berlin very well. In front of us a long stretch of the wall, full of graffiti of all colors, slogans, flowers, fun. It was from this platform that president Kennedy pronounced his famous "Ich bin ein Berliner!" (I am a Berliner) which gave strength and hope to West Berliners for a generation.

Our legs were so sore we couldn't make it all the way home without stopping in a *Stube* for a beer. In the evening we had *Wienerschnitzel* in the restaurant across the street and 2 more good German beers. This time, unlike in Vienna last February, we could even pay for a side order!

12 April 1980 – Both sides of Berlin and return to Poland

We were up and ready to go by 8 o'clock, we wanted to make the most of our last day in Germany. Our landlady served us a most welcome hearty breakfast and, while we ate, she kept telling us stories from her slowly fading but still lucid memories of the horrors of World War II: the air raids, especially. Like many older people she liked to talk and inevitably repeated herself. We heard some of it the other day too but it still sent shudders down our spines.

She wanted to convey to us, the future diplomats of the world, the horrors of wars. "The youth today do not realize," she said a few times. Of course, older people always say that young generations do not realize. This time, however, it actually rang true. I am not sure we really could realize, no matter how much history and international relations we studied.

The copious breakfast took time to consume. We were not in a hurry, both because it was tasty and because it gave us a chance to listen to more of her stories. In due course her loquacious narration took us to Berlin where our lady was displaced during the war. Here, under relentless Allied bombing, her 4-month old child starved to death in 1944. Her husband crazed when he returned from a prisoner of war camp. Her 17-year old son went to war too, though she did not say, and we did not dare to ask, whether he made it back alive.

She conveyed how fear replaced confidence as the Wehrmacht's successive defeats during the harsh winters on the Russian front slowly made it clear that Germany was doomed. She said she even tried to commit suicide by cutting her veins but did not do a good job and survived, alone, condemned to remember this tragedy for the rest of her life.

After taking leave from her I secretly shed a tear or two. She shared so many of her memories with us, and enriched our experience greatly, though she expressed no remorse, or even any doubts, about the actions of Nazi Germany. I would have liked to stay longer and listen to more of her stories, maybe ask her a few questions on how she felt about the Hitler and the Nazis. I would have liked to reciprocate her hospitality in some way, now or in the future, but I knew I would never see her again.

We moved back to East Berlin. Here we visited the Treptower Park, with another huge mausoleum to fallen Soviet soldiers. This time there were lots of locals, apparently it was a premium venue to get married and lots of young East German couples had their wedding photos taken during our visit. Obviously it was the politically correct thing to do.

We then took a walk along the wall, just of the other side of the Reichstag, which we could actually see over there, beyond the wall, the people and the cars in West Berlin. We took photos of each other touching the wall, hugging it while looking up at the borderless sky. Some buildings were split in two parts, a few apartments on one side, others on the other side. The eastern side of the wall was colorless, no graffiti were allowed.

By evening we were on a train again, heading east, and left Berlin and the wall behind us for one last time. The train was almost empty which allowed us plenty of room to relax and meditate on the divided city which had just hosted us and its symbolic significance in this tense time of the Cold War.

13 April 1980 – Walking and eating in Warsaw

In the morning all three of us went to the Wilanów park with Marzena. Unfortunately, while drinking tea in a *kawiarnia*, Ann's glass broke due to the hot water and she got wet pants. A walk in the fresh air dried them off but also made her feel sick and she was not able to finish our tour of the palace. We took her back to the dorm.

Ann would later relate how her friend Wadim was there and, after exchanging civilities, they began to badger each other about politics to the distress of roommate Halina. Ann asked him what was going on in the world, and he started to extol the merits of peace-loving Soviet Union, and then pointed out every nasty aggression the Americans were perpetrating around the world, including, bizarrely, military maneuvers in the *Tiergarten* in West Berlin. She told him we had just been there and there was no sign of any maneuvers, unless he considered scantily clad Berliners having picnics as a military threat. Hard to imaging he really believed what he was saying.

I wish I were there, I had NEVER heard ONE positive word about the Russians or the USSR from ANY Polish person I met in Poland to this day. Except if we were talking about drinking stamina, where the Russians were known to excel.

While Ann was enjoying the rare privilege of listening to pro-Soviet arguments by a Polish citizen, Andrew and I were invited to lunch at Marzena's place (needless to say we are again overfed with precious meats and other hard to find delicacies) and met her brother Marek.

We then went out for a walk in the old city. *Stare Miasto* was always charming, it had been rebuilt very well almost from scratch after the near total destruction of World War II. Marzena was a very friendly and smart young lady. She clearly wanted out of Poland, she saw no end to the dark days of socialist depression. So did her brother Marek, a soft-spoken and very handsome kid who would often tag along with us although his English was rather limited and we could not get into complex conversations with him.

She got visibly upset when, at about 8 o'clock in the evening, we told her we were really not hungry for another meal. It was the truth, we were still quite full from lunch. Sometimes we would try, unsuccessfully, to decline her dinner invitations because we knew it was difficult and expensive for her family to get a hold of all the goodies they kept offering to us. But there was nothing to do about it and we had to go and eat again. (And drink: vodka was never absent from the table.)

This extreme hospitality was not totally new to me. It was the same I found every time I visited my relatives in Calabria and Puglia. You had to eat everything all the time or else they would take umbrage. And if you ate at the home of one relative you automatically must eat at everyone else's, lest they took offense and didn't talk to you again. There was never any point trying to resist.

14 April 1980 – New Polish visa and ice cream

After our usual morning classes we once again had to attend the government visa office: our last Polish student visa had been cancelled because we left the country to go to Berlin. Why? Who knows, but must there be a reason? Maybe to provide a few more government jobs in the visa office. Whatever... Three more forms to fill out and two days to wait before we had return and pick up our passports adorned with one more blue Polish visa stamp.

The employee who was dealing with our stuff was amazed to find out that Ann spoke good Polish and was of partial Polish (and Slovak) origin, and started a long and complex conversation on Polish literature with her. I did not understand anything and had a feeling Ann did not always follow all the details either, but that was not the point. It was pretty amazing to see her carry on with total control of the situation. So the visit to the visa office took even longer than usual, but it was actually enjoyable, as far as a visit to a visa office in any country could ever be.

We had to fill out this new form but it was in Polish and when Ann went to the lady to ask her for a translation, she translated in simple Polish questions that were almost worse than those asked us at the Czech military base. She wanted to know the names, ages and occupations of every member of our immediate families.

Then she wanted to know how Ann had learned Polish and refused to believe she learnt it by myself in 3 months. She tried to chide her saying, "one must be very talented to learn a language by oneself so well in 3 months". Then she asked if she had ever read any Polish books and she told her they were too difficult. She then got a 5 minute lecture on how beautifully Sienkiewicz and Mickiewicz wrote and how she ought to read them.

Ann and I then went down to *Orbis* to talk to Mr. Głombinski, our travel agent. Great news: they had accepted our trip to Russia but have put us in hotels. It would cost 165 dollars per person. Ugh! Horribly expensive!

In the early evening, after the inevitable huge meal at Marzena's home, this time of home-made *pierogi* (dumplings of unleavened dough filled with different stuff and boiled, it was meat this time), we all went to a local park and played frisbee.

Frisbees were all over the place in American universities but still a novelty over here. After playing we sat down and, why I am not sure really, I started quoting Dante to Ann, reciting the poetic description of Caronte, the figure which carries souls to the underworld. We were on a bench on one side of the lake and saw Andrew and Marzena on the other side. We called to them just as five stray dogs ran up to them, barking in an excited state.

After having burned a lot of calories running after the disc, we proceeded to replace them back into our bodies by devouring excellent local ice cream! Polish ice cream was always readily available, very creamy and tasty, could compete with the best Italian ice cream and of course much cheaper.

15 April 1980 – Meals, music and socialist toilets

Instead of our usual Polish Political Systems lecture today, a man, a Mr. Myślik, came from the organization ZNAK to discuss church-state relations. ZNAK was the main catholic organization in Poland that was allowed to operate at the official level. It even had members in the national Parliament, the *Sejm*. It had to walk a fine line between loyalty to the pope in Rome and allegiance to the socialist state. It got in trouble in 1976 when it opposed a constitutional amendment that proclaimed eternal friendship with the USSR but it survived in various forms, including catholic clubs. The lecture was not really interesting, but it WAS interesting that they would allow one class to be taught by a ZNAK member.

After class, we met briefly with Bogdan. He had arranged to send Cathy a letter so she would not need to pay for her stay in Poland – that is to say the daily exchange of money mandatory for tourists. Bogdan was always very helpful, whenever he could he would try and make our life easier through the Polish bureaucracy, beyond his call of duty as organizer of our academic program.

Afternoon at home doing homework. Sort of. This curriculum was not very hard, really, much less so than our course load back at Georgetown. But that was not the point. We were here to experience much more importantly than to study. And we sure were experiencing beyond expectations, and learning much more than we ever could in a classroom!

Dinner again at Marzena's, where we were, as usual, hopelessly overfed. Her family's warmth and hospitality was beyond imagination. What puzzled us about their apartment was that there seemed to be only three rooms: a kitchen, a living room and a kind of smallish study. I innocently asked where they all slept and Marzena became rather flustered. I realized I should probably have kept my mouth shut and did not pursue the issue further.

We then all went to the *Sala Koncertowa* for a performance by the Academy of St. Martin in the Fields, a famous London-based chamber orchestra. They made a triumphal performance and were called back by the public for five encores.

After which, need I say?, we went back to Marzena's for a little night snack: cheese, cold cuts, bread (excellent Polish brown bread) and butter, everything irrigated with plenty of vodka. We were lucky that we were never tested for alcohol when driving home after one of these dinners.

Back at the dorm we met Stefan who had just returned from the USSR, from the Armenian Soviet Socialist Republic to be precise.

He had gone there to represent Poland at some international event for socialist youth organizations. He got to travel a lot in his capacity as head of the communist youth organization at the university.

He focused on practical aspects of his trip. He told us stories of how the student dormitory where he was housed in Yerevan, Armenia's capital, did not have toilet paper. In fact it did not have any real toilets, just holes in the ground. No hot water either, only cold water three hours per day. He did find one toilet for his use before returning however, it was at the airport. Bizarrely, he said there was a sign indicating that it was reserved for foreign travelers only, Soviet citizens were not admitted!

Why this was so remained beyond our understanding: the only explanation was that, toilets being scarce, the Armenian SSR authorities did not want to look dirty to foreigners. But toilets could not be that scarce, or expensive, to build at an international airport, even in Yerevan.

It was a refrain we would encounter often in socialist countries: the hated (by the regime) foreigner (often a capitalist, though not in this case) got "privileges" the members of the local proletariat, nominally in charge of the government and the economy, could not dream of.

As we chatted the evening away with some vodka and snacks, Stefan saw the pamphlet *Facts about Poland* which we had been given at school to study for our exams and commented drily: "You won't find any facts in there, not a word of truth".

16 April 1980 – Mail and telephone

Today we had another lecture in Marxist economics with our professor Wincenty Kaminski. He was a very pale, sandy haired, good looking man with a rather weird demeanor. His pupils were pinpoints which gave him the look of being absent from the room, as in a world of his own, or on drugs. Probably the former. His tone of voice was rather monotonous, he certainly did not look like he was enjoying himself with us. During the whole course, he never smiled.

By chance, we met Stefan again at the university. He looked at our books on the economics of the socialist countries and said, much along the lines of his comments last night: "All lies". He usually spoke with a low voice, with no intonation, succinct and to the point. He was clearly a man of the system but also someone who was aware of the problems and wanted to change it. Of course, he could be acting, perhaps to test our reactions, but I was convinced he was sincere.

In the afternoon Ann and I picked up our passports at the police station on Krucza street. The woman there was getting to know us well. She asked first if Ann had yet bought any Polish books as she had kind of promised she would the last time we were here. Sorry. In the afternoon Ann came to my room to write Cathy a long letter and attached her VISA authorization letter. All was In order, it looked like we would be able to get her over here after all!

In the evening I wanted to go and visit Ewa together with Marzena. As I picked her up at home, I was invited to another – you guess – unnecessarily abundant but irresistibly tasty dinner. After which we drove to Ewa's apartment but she was not at home.

Private telephone lines were not always to be taken for granted in Poland, even in the capital city. Therefore sometimes the only way to communicate with someone was to go to their home, and if they were out, well try again another time! International calls were even more difficult. I had to go to the post office every time I needed to call Italy. Rather annoying.

I could have been wrong but did not think it was a matter of cost, but rather of control: if everyone had a phone line it would be impossible to bug them all! (Although East Germany's secret police had shown they could come pretty close!) And some people, like Marian and Ewa, could certainly afford a phone line, but I suspected they did not want to have one to avoid being bugged.

17 April 1980 – Sending letters abroad

Even sending letters abroad was not easy. This morning Ann and I got up early and at 6:30am went to the airport to ask someone, anyone, whom we could see traveling to the United States to post her letter to Cathy once across the Atlantic. Ann found a cooperative gentleman in the check-in line for the flight to New York.

She approached him with an envelope in her hand and had to say no more. He understood exactly what she was going to ask him to do: he picked up the envelope and spoke to us reassuringly, he would post it as soon as he got to the United States. Precious papers for Cathy's visa which absolutely had to reach her or she would not be able to join us.

We learned that this was common practice for expats living in Warsaw. The Polish authorities could, in theory, have asked to submit all these letters to censorship the same way that they censored mail posted to and from Poland to western countries. But they did not.

Posting from Poland might take ages and many letters were "lost". Many letters were stamped "damaged in transportation", ie opened by the censors to make sure the content was acceptable then sealed again with some tape. Several letters I received from home during my stay fell in the latter category. I suppose they had some good Italian speakers in the censorship department, and some calligraphy experts to decipher the terrible hand writing of my mother. I always forgot to ask her if the letters I wrote to Italy were also "damaged in transportation".

The airport trip was very fast so Ann and I had time to spare before class so we went for breakfast at the Forum Hotel. Later in the day Ann came over to our room and while Andrew and I studied, she caught up on her sleep. We went out for dinner to the restaurant *Ulubiona* and later Ann and I sat for a long time on the windowsill overlooking Madalinskiego street from the third floor discussing the meaning of life. So romantic with a view of the bullet holes from World War II still visible on the building in front of us.

18 April 1980 – Shopping, smoking and tea

There was a horrible drilling noise above the classroom where our lectures were held. Mr. Roszkowski, our history professor, went upstairs to see if they couldn't do that a little more quietly and came back down with the response "The Five Year Plan must be fulfilled". We had to move to another building. After class, he confided to Ann that he wanted her to know there were certain things, like Katyn, about which it is forbidden to talk. That is why rooms like this were better for that purpose: the noise would made everyone freer to talk.

After class we went downtown, to the *Centrum* shopping mall. There was very little to shop. I was looking for light summer clothing, a jacket and some shirts with short sleeves, but no luck. What was available was cheap but so depressingly dreary that even someone like me who knew little about clothing and cared less ended up not buying anything at all.

In the afternoon it was foreign policy classes again. Usual propaganda nonsense, I began to get a bit impatient at having to suffer through hours of party-line pre-packaged slogans. But the professors, most of them retired diplomats, were very polite and soft spoken.

One of them, Dr Tomorowych, a former ambassador of Poland to the United Nations, asked politely whether we would mind if he smoked. Andrew immediately said yes of course it was not a problem, and we all nodded. I was not too happy but what to do? We were guests in his office and most Poles smoked pretty much everywhere, whether it was allowed or not, at home or at work, with guests or clients, or students for that matter. There was nothing like the relentless campaigns we had in the west to raise awareness of the negative health consequences of smoking.

He then started to light up a long, uninterrupted series of really awfully acrid and bitter cigarettes for the whole duration of the class. By the time we got out we emanated a stinky stench all around us, the smoke had impregnated our clothes and would stay with us for the rest of the day.

At some point during the class Ann was not feeling well (maybe because of the smoke which had filled the room?) and our professor went over and bought her some medicine. The gallantry of Polish men never ceased to astound the lady among us.

Later we were invited by Pat, the American student who had joined the Georgetown program at our university, to go to the American Embassy for a drink at the "Marines' bar". A strange place where "eastern" people were not admitted and US marines got drunk mostly among themselves since they were not allowed to socialize with local girls. We politely turned down the less than irresistibly enticing offer.

In the evening it was tea time at the home of Larissa, Marzena's best friend. Her family seemed to be doing well, the point of having bought her this house, in addition to owning their own. Her father was a successful diplomat, and had been posted to the United States. Larissa lived alone in a three-bedroom house in Łazenki, a (relatively) posh neighborhood of the capital. Not quite what you would expect from the daughter of a diplomat of a socialist regime but whatever, she was a pleasant young woman and we spent an enjoyable evening together.

19 April 1980 – Football and mountain climbing

Easy day. Tried to go to a bank but it was closed. Sometimes they were open on Saturdays, but not on this Saturday: it was a Free Saturday or *Wolna Sobota*. Basically a Saturday off, like having two Sundays in a row. Later I visited the post office to make a phone call to Italy. I had to wait half an hour or so for my turn. I had the time to reflect that it must be easier to call the moon.

Easy afternoon at Larissa's home watching Italy vs Poland, a friendly soccer match. Not so exciting, it ended with an inconclusive 2-2. Anyway better, for Italy, than the bitter day when we lost to Poland in 1974 and were eliminated from the World Cup in West Germany. The memory of that match was occasionally still painful in my soccer fan heart.

After the match Marzena gave us no choice: her mother had prepared dinner for us and we were expected to show up very soon. Again, an avalanche of proteins, cold and hot, were spread over the dining table by the time we arrived in the simple apartment to take our seats.

During dinner we watched some TV and there was a program on mountaineering. The whole country was justifiably proud that a Polish expedition had reached the summit of Mount Everest in February of this year, the first team ever to make it in winter. Leska Cichy and Krzysztof Wielicki, two young mountaineers had become national heroes.

It was, appropriately for the occasion, unseasonably cold in Warsaw. When we left Marzena's place to drive back to our dorms it was snowing!

20 April 1980 – Stripping at a wedding

Today we had a strange chat with Natalia, a friend of Ann's who lived in her same dorm. Somehow we started talking about her recent wedding party and she told us how the celebrations had been somewhat unusual. People got a bit drunk and started to strip until some were totally naked. Some guests rushed to cover up the naked men (women apparently were more reluctant to lay themselves bare), but she did not mind to see that at her wedding. It made it all seem more natural, she said.

She said her was not an isolated case. I was aware that going naked was something that was sometimes used in Communist countries as a display of protest. Not many other ways of protesting were allowed and this was a cheap and cheerful one. In East Germany they were especially good at it: being naked in public was one of the few (the only?) somehow transgressive activity that was permitted by the Communist party. I am not sure there was anything political in these Poles getting naked, probably not, but surely they wanted to do something unusual.

One of the worst consequences of the socialist system was the homogeneity that was forced upon people. The general ideal of equality, which we could all agree to if it meant equality of opportunity, was implemented in a way that the result was a boring sameness. Everyone was not necessarily equal to his neighbor but was often the same: same clothes, same apartments, same cars, same food. The result was a flattened, boring society. So many Poles were trying to be different, to stand out, to find their own individual self in whatever way they could.

I spent the afternoon in my room studying for the upcoming exams. But I did not study too long and not too hard. Romek came up to visit and invited us to go out for a beer, so we all went to the *Bolek* pub. I downed one beer, some of my classmates up to five or six. We had very open and candid conversations about all kinds of subjects. It was really amazing how we had become close friends with Polish students in such a short time. I guess it was in part because of their eagerness to meet people from the West, and our eagerness to tear up the Iron Curtain. Beer and vodka did a lot to facilitate our integration with the new friends and acquaintances.

In the evening we were again invited to eat at Marzena's, our second home in Warsaw by now. Our first, really, if we consider where we were most welcome at any time on any day and where we ate most of our food! Simple cooking, lots of proteins and fat, cabbages, cheeses, bread. I guess the only thing that sometimes I left on the plate was chunks of pure pork fat, of which by now we had already digested more during our time in Poland than in the rest of our previous and future time on this planet put together.

In fact, judging from the voracity of our appetite at every meal, I would have to say everything must have been very good. We were really very lucky to be treated like royals every day we came here, which was almost every day.

Her mother had already cooked a duck. A week ago we had bet a duck that Poland would win yesterday's match against Italy but it turned out to be a tie. Marzena's mother cooked the duck anyway, even though Poland didn't lose. The duck had crispy skin and tender juicy meat.

21 April 1980 – Private lodging

In the evening we all went to the Chopin Academy for a concert by the famous Italian pianist Ruggero Gerlin. He was getting on with age and showed it but still played quite well.

During a conversation with Ann a few days ago I had argued that one could not love the music of both Beethoven (my idol) and Chopin. But I had to admit I was wrong: one could. After a few Chopin concerts in Warsaw, I did. One additional reason why my stay in Poland was turning out to be so educational![18]

Afterwards Ann and I went to Ewa and Marian to pick up the keys to an apartment of some friends of theirs where I would host my parents who were planning to visit soon. Strictly speaking it was illegal to rent out private apartments to foreigners for hard currency payments, but of course it was a widespread practice among Poles with a little extra real estate to spare.

Obviously I would pay in dollars for this and for the owners it was going to be a significant boost to their income for the month. Who was the actual owner in fact we had no idea, but a set of keys had somehow been entrusted to the capable hands of a hot lady friend of Ewa's who used the apartment to meet some anonymous rich Italian man who lavished her with gifts. Of course, we would never know more, and did not need to.

---

18 *Nevertheless, Beethoven would remain my idol forever: for one thing we have the same birthday, and moreover his family originated in the Flanders (hence the prefix "van" in his last name), from the village of Mechelen, just a few kilometers from my home of over twenty years.*

We then went to have a look at the apartment: a fairly dreadful grey building, typical Soviet-style cinderblock construction. But everything was in order, it was big enough for the purpose and clean.

22 April 1980 – Classes and some privacy

Usual routine classes in the morning at SGPiS. We were moving along with our curricula and were getting ready for the final exams.

In the afternoon another international relations class at the foreign policy institute. By and large we were at the receiving end of a predictable flow of propaganda but I reflected that while I was initially impatient these classes were actually becoming kind of fun. Not because of what the professors told us and wanted (or pretended they wanted) us to learn.

It was interesting to see how educated professional bent reality to suit the mandatory party line. They actually did a pretty good job of it. Basically they zig-zagged between "well you know we did not like doing it but we had to do it because the USSR so decided and left us no choice" and "we had to do it and it actually made at least some sense, in a way, if you think about it from another point of view".

Spent the night at the apartment I rented for my parents, they wouldn't arrive for another couple of days but the landlord was kind enough to give me the keys a few days in advance for free. Nice to be away from the student dorm, privacy and space. After all I had never had a whole apartment all for myself in my life, in any country!

24 April 1980 – Dad and mum come to Poland

After the usual morning classes and lunch, in the early afternoon I drove Giallina to the city's airport, which was proudly named after Fryderyck Chopin, to pick up my parents who were flying in from Rome to visit for a week.

I anticipated that it was going to be a week of surprises for them, their first time ever in any country behind the "iron curtain". They were obviously very happy to see me and excited about visiting. They flew with Lot, the Polish flag carrier. Alitalia did not operate a flight to Warsaw. They said the Soviet-made aircraft was not especially comfortable and the service on board left a lot to be desired, but the flight was only a couple of hours long, no big deal.

They arrived on time and after quickly going through border formalities I took them to the rented apartment so they could freshen up.

In the evening, Andrew and Ann took all of us out for a meal of duck at our "1st duck place" as we referred to the anonymous little restaurant near the old town market square where we had consumed many a duck in recent weeks. We named it so in order to distinguish it from the "2nd duck place", a similar eatery also in the center of Warsaw. Who knows why duck was so popular on Polish menus.

25 April 1980 – A flower, a blind singer and a party

Today it was my name day and Ann bought me a flower. Name day celebrations are taken more seriously here than in the West, though in Italy some older people still remember, its origin has got to do with religion: a name day is not just a name attached to a day, it is the day when a particular saint is celebrated. So today is Saint Mark's day.

Be that as it may, I am pretty sure it was the first flower I ever received from a girl! I was quite pleased and especially very surprised, hopefully it won't be the last. I am not a good flower giver myself, I would have to work on it.

During the afternoon we attended a party at SGPiS that had been organized for the participants in an East-West trade seminar that was taking place this week. Our university was relatively open to broadening international contacts with the whole world, irrespective of ideology. The substance of the seminar was not so important as the opportunity for young colleagues from the two sides of the Cold War to mingle together and speak freely.

We were not official participants: those came in formal delegations from the many countries represented: member states of the European Economic Community (EEC), Comecon, North America. But everyone seemed to be eager to have us around. It seemed any opportunity to associate with westerners was precious for most of our Polish colleagues. And we too were very eager to be here. We could hear more candid talk, and learn more about politics and economics, in this kind of context that in any classroom.

Lots of flags were hanging from the balconies in the inner courtyard of the university. I wished I could take some of the flags home for my collection but no chance. (Just kidding.) The flags were hanging in no special order, and the American and the Italian flag happened to be next to each other, how appropriate for the three of us!

In the evening we all went to the home of Karol, a blind singer. It was amazing how he could not only sing but actually have a very positive attitude to life despite his circumstances. He could sing in English as well as Polish.

I ended up staying out late with some friends and went back to our room number 325 before midnight. Andrew went with Ann, Marzena and her brother Marek to a ballroom dance, where they enjoyed XIX century style dancing until the early morning. Because we did not coordinate Andrew ended up being locked out of the dorm! The dorm door was locked at midnight but this was never a problem, a little tip to the chubby porter and we were always let in.

But today somehow the lady, a gargantuan lady who never smiled, was not around. Or maybe she was, but fast asleep. The next day I woke up and saw an empty bed and felt sorry for Andrew, but then I thought oh well not too bad, stuff like that can happen and I guessed he was most probably in good company, with no shortage of kanapki and vodka.

26 April 1980 – East-West seminar

Today was the final day of the seminar on East-West Trade at SGPiS. Andrew participated in a panel chaired by Krzystof, one of our friends, to which he had been invited at short notice. That was a great opportunity for active involvement in the event, and it was quite interesting even if to some extent predictable.

Ann and I were supposed to have lunch with my parents at the *Staropolska*. She took the bus into the city to meeet us, disembarked before the gates to Warsaw University, and evidently struck one man so much that he began to follow her, bought her flowers, proposed marriage, told her he could not offer her much money but he could offer her eternal happiness.

She thought about it for a second or two, it's not every day any woman gets an offer like that, but eventually decided to decline. He kissed her hands a dozen times before letting her go to lunch. She told me, from a woman's point of view, how Polish men were always so romantic in a XIX century way a modern western woman could be briefly stunned before realizing this was 1980 and it was all so surreal.

In the evening we were invited to a ball that had been thrown for seminar participants. We sat at a table with the Russian delegation. Later on, Ann and I went to Krystof's apartment with Marina and Koliya from the Leningrad delegation. The blind guy, Karol, played his guitar. I soon became bored and wanted to go while Ann found the Russian company fascinating and wanted to stay. I think the reason was a tall handsome Russian guy who showered her with his effusive compliments while the Russian ladies were not really paying any attention to me, but I could be wrong.

27 April 1980 – Wilanow, missed Chopin and lots of food

In the morning we all went to *Wilanow*, a beautiful park with a magnificent royal palace from the XVII century. We were lucky as it was a beautiful sunny day. Long walks and visit to the palace, heritage of the time when Poland was a powerful kingdom during the age of the Enlightenment. The palace was designed in the 1670s by Augustyn Locci, a Polish architect of Italian descent whose parents had emigrated to Poland a few years earlier. The palace itself was conceived in Royal French style, much like Versailles, while the garden was the typical Italian style of the time.

Lunch at Marzena's, where we witnessed some funny exchanges between my parents and hers since they had no common language and no one in the room could translate from Italian to Polish beyond my basic introductions. So the conversation developed via English. They would speak to me in Italian, I would translate into English, and Ann would relay in Polish, and vice versa. Much was probably lost in translation, but who cared about the substance, it was a very warm welcome and a meeting between two sets of parents of college kids with very different backgrounds and expectations, and all appreciated this opportunity very much.

After lunch we went to stretch our legs at *Zelanowa Wola*, the birthplace of Chopin. Unfortunately his home/museum was closed, despite the fact that Marzena had called them in advance to make sure they would be open to visitors. Too bad. We promised to ourselves that we would try to come back, it was not far and there were frequent concerts performed by pianists from all over the world.

Dinner back to Marzena's. My parents had a hard time understanding when Ann, Andrew and I tried to explain that in order to buy even basic food people had to line up outside shops for hours, with no guarantee there would be any food left when they reached the counter. Marzena's family provided such opulent meals that they made you think this was easy. Of course it was not, we knew well, and it was all the more remarkable for that.

We had driven around town a lot today and needed to fill up Giallina's tank one more time. For the first time, our usual gas station would not sell us fuel at the "Polish" price, apparently they had some problems with the police. Therefore today they wanted the "foreign" price, about four times more expensive for us.

No problem, undeterred we just drove to another station and proceeded as usual to pay the "local" price plus a little mark-up for the pockets of the gas station's boss: 25 zl/liter.

28 April 1980 – Studying and cooking

Usual classes at school in the morning, then to my parents' apartment to study. They went to Krakow for a couple of days so I could take advantage of the extra space and privacy. In all honesty I could not seriously argue I was studying hard. The program was nowhere nearly as challenging as Georgetown's courses in Washington. But again, that's not why we were here.

After studying I was joined by Ann who had spent the afternoon doing her own homework in her dorm. I cooked some Italian sauce (with local produce, it was not quite the same thing but not too bad in the end). Especially the tomatoes left a bit to be desired. They were not Italian for sure and there was no label to tell their provenance. They were probably from Bulgaria, or some other brotherly socialist country with more sunshine than Poland. Luck has it that Italian food, at least in its basic concepts, is fairly easy to learn and cook even with foreign ingredients. I found a bottle of cheap wine in some shop I ran into by chance to make it a real dinner.

It was relaxing to be able to spend time in a real apartment, for a change, but I preferred Marzena's excessive meals, both for the quality of the food prepared by her mother and, especially, for the human experience of spending time with her loving family.

29 April 1980 – Dinner, party and flags

Busy all day with classes, in the morning at SGPiS and in the afternoon at the foreign policy center. We were not done before 7:15 in the evening. The three of us then went to the apartment and met my parents, who had returned from Krakow, as well as Ewa and Marian, whom we invited to the *Budapest* restaurant for dinner. Hearty Hungarian fare. So cheap... 3,300 złoty (some 120 dollars) for a full meal in a luxury restaurant for 7 people, including 2 bottles of excellent Spanish wine. Marian and Ewa were more critical than usual (which is to say something) of the system, and it seemed clear that they were planning to emigrate from Poland, where they saw no future.

After dinner my parents went to sleep. Andrew took Marzena out for a walk while Ann and I went to meet some Russian students at a party, and we stayed up and had fun until about 1:00 in the morning. Interesting, even surprising cultural experience, it was the first time we associated with Russians for a whole night in a relatively free environment and could speak quite freely about anything. (It would also be one of the last.)

One Russian lady, Marina, said she was totally, absolutely in love with Lenin. She talked all night about Lenin as if he were some kind of Father Christmas. She sang a song that she said was Lenin's favorite tune. She was almost in tears as she did... Maybe she believed in what she was saying. Maybe she was a Communist Party minder, there was almost always one with Soviet citizens who were allowed to interact with western colleagues. Or maybe she was not a minder but wanted to impress the group's minder by performing the role of a devoted communist in front of western colleagues, that would possibly earn her points toward a future trip abroad.

It was always hard to say, with Soviet students, how much they really believed what they said and how much they had to say it, perhaps because their party custodian angel was looking over their shoulders. Yet, what a stark difference between them and the Poles. In over two months here, I had yet to meet a single Polish student, just ONE, who professed to be a communist believer, let alone one who would volunteer to sing Lenin songs!

After the party, Ann and I raided the city for Polish flags. I liked to collect flags from the countries I visited, and most of the time I bought them. But they mean so much more if you can "borrow" them from some remarkable building, or on some important occasion. These days Warsaw was covered with flags in preparation for Labor Day, the all-important May 1st celebrations, so charged with ideological significance. So it was easy to just pick them off government buildings, party headquarters, schools, banks, dorms, you name it, they had a flag.

I especially wanted one big beautiful flag adorning a hospital. It was hoisted a tad too high for even tall Ann to reach. So, since I was stronger, I moved some heavy blocks that were lying around under the flag. Ann, since she was taller, jumped up a few times and brought the flag tumbling down. She kindly gave it to me as my name day (April 25th) gift.

Luckily no one was around. Later, thinking about it, I realized we had been very silly indeed in risking it. How embarrassing if the police had seen us. We could have jeopardized our whole semester's program. I would have had to call my folks in Krakow to tell them I had been caught red-handed and was now languishing in a cold jail. A nightmare.

We just took four big flags. Two were just plain and simple flags, red and white, a couple had a coat of arms with an eagle painted on the top left corner. (I wondered why so many countries chose an eagle for their coat of arms, flags, seals, etc. Insignia designers are not an imaginative lot.) Anyway it would be good publicity for Poland when we put them up on the wall in our dorm rooms back home in Washington D.C., so we did not feel so guilty.

30 April 1980 – Nourishing body and mind

Last day of classes. It had not been a hard semester, let me say it once more. But it had been and would probably remain the most instructive semester of all our years in university. What we learned living in Poland, meeting our colleagues and just experiencing life here could not possibly be taught. It was priceless.

Out for lunch with parents, then some shopping. One of the few items of high-end manufacturing quality and reasonable prices you could find in the official, non-black market stores was crystal. I loved crystal and in the *Stare Miasto* we could find a few shops that sold beautiful vases for 1,300 to 1,800 złoty, less than fifty US dollars. Parents bought a few to take back to Rome.

The evening saw us going to the *Wielicki Teatr* (Big Theater) for a ballet performance. For two centuries this had been the most prestigious opera and ballet theaters in the country. It was not really possible to find tickets in the open market. And I did not really look into the black market. Our head teacher Bogdan, however, who had been taking such good care of us ever since we arrived last February, somehow found them and very kindly provided them to us! I did not ask how he did it, but he did it. The ballet was good, but the orchestra was a really fine ensemble and we had very good seats.

After the performance we invited Bogdan and his wife to the Victoria hotel for a dinner at the *Canaletto* restaurant. It was always a sublime experience to come and dine here. Food, service, ambiance... everything was perfect. Again it was all quite cheap (for us!) including a couple of bottles of Grignolino d'Asti from Italy and lots of meat for everyone and all for less than 75 dollars for the six of us. We had a pleasant conversation with Bogdan and his very outspoken wife, a smart and beautiful woman who did not have an official position and was therefore less restrained in her criticism of the Polish political system.

1 May 1980 – International Workers' Day celebrations

Unfortunately today my folks had to fly home. So they would miss the elaborate celebrations of international workers' day. This is a festivity observed in many countries around the world, but is especially charged with ideological *gravitas* in a socialist country. Preparations had been underway for several days and the city was full of fancy decorations, ideological banners, big red flags and red stars of all sizes. Ann had to miss the celebrations as well as she fell sick last night, perhaps our schedule of partying was too punishing for her physique.

After taking my parents to the airport I returned to school and joined the large contingent of SGPiS students for a long walk to downtown. Hundreds of thousands of people from all walks of life converged to the Marszałkowska avenue and paraded in front of a grand stand at the center of which stood no less than Edward Gierek, General Secretary of the United Workers' Party of Poland (the longwinded official name of the Communist Party), the whole Politburo of the party, government ministers, foreign ambassadors etc. It was interesting to see the lineup on the stand, as the exact position of each official was directly related to his/her (not many women though, in fact I did not see any in the top leadership) rank in the hierarchy. Stefan was with them, as representative of the students! Warsaw was red today.

The sky however was blue, a glorious warm sunny day (finally, finally!!) which made it possible for many not just to pay tribute to the workers of the world but also to enjoy a day out, with people singing, dancing, eating and drinking as they moved along.

I took lots of pictures. At one point I wanted to take a picture of Andrew with his arms raised up in a parody of surrender in front of the headquarters of the communist party. It looked a bit sarcastic, though we meant no evil. Plus, we had been mocking the party aloud and maybe the police nearby heard and understood us? Unlikely, I think they just saw foreign-looking kids and wanted to feel important and deploy their power. Anyway a zealous officer who was guarding the building approached me and wanted the roll of my camera.

I was a bit upset, not so much for the picture of Andrew in front of this ugly building (we could always come back and take another one on a quieter day!), but because I would lose all the other irreplaceable pictures of the day. So I started arguing with him. After a few minutes Marzena showed up and persuaded him to let us go. Phew... Once again her persuasive powers with the police had extracted me from trouble!

In the evening Ann and I went back to my parents' rented flat to study for our exams. The owner kindly left us the keys for an extra day after the agreed lease was over. At 11pm we were hungry and I prepared some spaghetti *all'arrabbiata* (literally "angry pasta"): tomato sauce with some olive oil, lots of spicy red chili and garlic. I usually liked it with some parsley or basil leaves, but could not find any today. A red hot evening to appropriately see off a very red day!

3 May 1980 – Telephones in the dorm

Full day studying for the upcoming exams. Easy stuff. The afternoon was interrupted by Ewa's call: she needed to return the apartment's keys back to the landlord. Oh well, too bad it was nice to have my own flat in central Warsaw.

We did not have a private telephone in our dorm rooms of course, only a common telephone in the corridor. When we received a call someone of goodwill had to pick up and alert the person being called by knocking on his door and yelling: "Telephone!!"

Or take a message. We never picked up the phone because we hardly ever received a call, and anyway it would have been difficult to understand unless the calling party spoke English. So in a way we were telephone free riders. But most colleagues seemed happy to do us this favor, and guessing the name of the interlocutors and the content of other people's phone calls made for some fun gossip among the students.

Andrew and I returned the keys of the flat used by my parents in the evening. Always a good opportunity to have a chat with Marian and Ewa and catch up with their not-sugar-coated vision of the socialist world.

4 May 1980 – End of an era in Yugoslavia

Full day at the dorm reading for our exams. Except, of course, for a long lunch break at Marzena's. As usual, we were treated to a wide array of hard to find animal proteins, tasty bread and this time also a few veggies, though I tried to be careful with my alcohol intake so as not to unnecessarily jeopardize the academic achievements of my studying later in the afternoon.

We heard some news which was very relevant to our studies: Jozif Broz Tito, the long-time communist ruler of Yugoslavia, had died today. Maybe today, or maybe a while ago: he had been on the brink for some time and the news coming from Belgrade was not always complete or verifiable. The leadership had been releasing information on his health at a deliberate pace for some time, to avoid any unpredictable reactions in the country and outside.

Things would never be the same in Yugoslavia, and were likely to change between Yugoslavia and the rest of the Socialist camp, not necessarily for the better. I wondered whether the USSR, strong of its initial success in Afghanistan over the last few months, might be tempted to reassert its control in neutral, but still nominally communist, Yugoslavia, under the usual pretext of heeding the call for help of fellow socialists under threat of reactionary restoration.

Tito was also a leader of the so-called "non-aligned movement", a collection of countries which tried to position themselves between the capitalist circle of American allies and the socialist block led by the USSR. India, Indonesia and Yugoslavia were among the most important ones, with many others mostly in Africa and Asia. Cuba was also a member, though it had unsurprisingly argued for a long time that "non-aligned countries" should have been naturally aligned with the USSR and against American imperialism. Without Tito, the movement, too, would never be the same. We were going to witness interesting times ahead.

5 May 1980 – Informal lecture on the Polish political system

In the morning we had our history exam. The question was "Communist takeover in eastern European communist countries". The wording of the question was a bit convoluted, even recursive. Also, it was a political question much more than a historical one. I wrote down a fairly plain vanilla answer. To write what I really thought would have been perceived as provocative. To write what we had been taught in class would have been a farce and totally lacking in self esteem.

In the evening I was in my room studying for the next exam, which would be on "Socialist political systems", when Stefan popped in and told me not to waste any time with my class notes. Things were not like what they taught us. He sat down and went on for a long time with a most interesting monologue on his views of "real" politics in Poland, ie on how the HQ of the Communist party decided everything and sent down orders, all the way to the lowliest head of a small party cell in the countryside, through the chain of command of "democratic centralism".

This was the decision-making mechanism in use in all communist parties, whether in power in east Europe or, mostly, in opposition in the west. Decision on policy, or on executive appointments, were made at the top, then passed down to lower levels of the hierarchy for approval. Of course, since the top leadership was the expression of the people's will, by definition there was no need for alternative policies or candidates to be taken into consideration.

Take any policy: a single proposal would be put on the ballot by the top leadership. The lower levels could only approve, whether they agreed or not. If they did not, they could cross the single proposal coming from the top and write down an alternative. But they could never put their alternative on the ballot from the start and could not really campaign for it. Which meant, for all practical purposes, the official proposal was all but certain to be approved.

This system was not a secret, it was openly detailed in the laws of the land and the statute of the party, but it had not been explained to us in class, as if our professors had tried to avoid embarrassment.

Most interesting indeed, even if I would not be able to use this information in the exam tomorrow. But who cared? I learned more tonight from Stefan about the political system of Poland and the other socialist countries than in all of our university classes put together.

6 May 1980 – Studying Comecon

In the morning we went for our Political Systems exam, very easy. In the afternoon I studied the economic relations among the member countries of the Council for Mutual Economic Assistance (CMEA, dubbed *Comecon* for "Communist economies"). This was once believed to be the USSR's response to the western European Common Market. In reality, it had always been anything but. Despite Soviet subsidies, countries were members of the CMEA because they had to, not because they wanted to. Never seen so much nonsense concentrated in so few pages like in our course material.

The official line was that socialist member states got together to develop their brotherly friendship in a way that would go beyond the vile capitalist trade, which was based on cold market prices and selfish profits. Sounded idealistic enough, except that, predictably, it did not work. Taking the profit motive away meant that huge inefficiencies inhibited trade, rather than enhancing it. A lot of the most important trade was in any case regulated bilaterally between each pair of countries, rather than multilaterally in the CMEA.

The Soviet Union used trade for political goals. Strong of its huge reserves of energy raw materials, it provided cheap hydrocarbons to the others to help guarantee a decent standard of living and prevent social turmoil. For the same purpose it bought low quality manufactured goods from them which could not be sold on the world market. It worked, in most of the satellite countries, most of the time. When it did not (Hungary 1956, Czechoslovakia 1968) Moscow sent in the tanks to put everyone back in their place.

Many countries wanted to join the nine members of the western EEC, there was a waiting list and no country ever left once they joined.[19] Not one European country I was aware of wanted to join the CMEA, while more than one member state would have likely left already if they had had a chance to do so. Albania actually did, but then its geographical position and Yugoslavia's anti-Soviet stance protected it from the danger of Warsaw Pact invasion.

8 May 1980 – Foreign Policy Exam

Morning at home studying, then light lunch (sort of light) with bread and sausages we got from Marian and Ewa.

There was not much meat readily available in Poland, not expensive choice cuts anyway. But sausages (*kiełbasa!*) had been our best friends for many meals. Cheap and almost always easily found in shops, they went very well with dark thick slices of Polish bread and savory butter. And vodka of course, though not today, since we had to write an exam in Polish foreign policy this afternoon.

Not that it would make much of a difference, give the kind of exam that awaited us: easy. Too easy, not challenging at all. I got 4 out of 5: in his remarks the professor noted that I had underestimated the extent to which revisionists in West Germany wanted to get back land that was now Poland. Of course such fringes were extremely marginal in West Germany, but politically very useful for the Polish regime to justify its alliance with Moscow in anti-German terms. I got a feeling that for him World War II was not yet completely over. This exam came at a very appropriate time considering what we would witness tomorrow.

---

19 *The first country to decide to leave the EEC, which by then had evolved into a broader European Union, would be the United Kingdom, through a referendum in 2016.*

9 May 1980 – Thirty-five Years of Victory

It was a big day today in Poland, another major celebration just a few days after Labor's Day: the 35th anniversary of the surrender of Nazi Germany in World War II. Many countries suffered because of the war, but Poland could reasonably claim to have endured the worst.

Poland had always felt the squeeze between Germany (or Prussia) and Russia (whether imperial or Soviet). For over a century Poland did not exist as a state, as it had been carved up by the two (with a sizable bite going to Austria). That was a pretty unenviable position to be in 1939, between the USSR and Germany, Stalin and Hitler, Communism and Nazism.

These days, of course, it was the fight against Nazi Germany that took center stage. And for sure that was what detonated World War II in Europe. Germany inflicted unspeakable human and economic damage to Poland between 1939 and 1945. More so to Polish Jews.

The Soviet attack that immediately followed the German invasion on 1 September 1939, however, got very short shrift. The official propaganda sang the praise of the heroic Soviet army that resisted German aggression and then moved to counterattack and liberate Poland (and Czechoslovakia, and Hungary, and Romania etc.) from fascism.

Of course, all but the most naive Poles knew that is far from the whole truth. Yes, the USSR did play a crucial role in defeating Germany but it received indispensable help from the United States through the "lend-lease" program and, as soon as the war was over, proceeded to occupy and subjugate the same countries to its own version of tyranny.

Also of course, they knew of Stalin's territorial ambitions in Poland, Katyn, lack of action during the Warsaw uprising. But they were not allowed to talk about it, not these days in communist Poland where no one was really a communist but censorship, and self-censorship, were tight.

10 May 1980 – Trip to Krakow

Not sure whether to spell it Cracow with two Cs or Krakow with two Ks. I had seen both. Somehow I preferred Krakow, it looked more

Polish. After an early breakfast we met with our professor Bogdan and Marzena. Bogdan had organized a minivan to take us to the second most important city in Poland. He kindly agreed to let us take Marzena with us. We felt this was a way to repay her, even if very partially, for her family's generosity and hospitality.

We spent the whole day in the vehicle, a rickety product of the Skoda factory in Czechoslovakia, I think, but I was not sure. It was equipped with uncomfortably hard shock absorbers and was quite slow, not that you could go very fast anyway on the Polish "highways" anyway, but it did the job. Reliable and not too noisy.

Short break on the way at Jaskinia Raj (Paradise Cave) to view some pretty impressive karst (rock formations caused by the dissolution of soluble minerals) caves full of stalactites and stalagmites. It was apparently Poland's most beautiful cave compex, and it attracted a fair number of visitors. They were only discovered in the early 1960s and had been opened to the public for less than ten years, it was still a novelty for most Poles.

It is always a bit eerie to walk into these caves, I remembered the first ones I saw, in Puglia, in southern Italy, at Castellana Grotte, a few years ago. Except there were many more people in Castellana. Here it was pretty empty and dark, it felt anything but a paradise to be honest. Maybe closer to a definition of hell if we had to remain down here too long! Just kidding, we did enjoy the visit, the view was dramatic and just thinking of the millions of years it took nature to make all this was awesome.

Later we stopped for a quick lunch break at Kielce, nothing to write home about, just a technical stop. We finally reached Krakow by the late afternoon. The evening started well with an excellent dinner at the restaurant of the hotel *Cracovia* (spelled with two Cs). Lots of tasty and hearty food, especially meat, fresh and cured, hot and cold, fatty and very fatty. Beer and a little vodka helped us digest the abundant proteins.

We then decided to try a local disco, but it was a dark and stinky lair, overcrowded and way too smoky. We ran away after less than five minutes inside. Much better to take a walk around the beautifully preserved old town. Krakow had been occupied by the Nazi throughout the war, art treasures were looted and the Jews were first confined to a ghetto, then deported to extermination camps. However the city did not suffer the fate of Warsaw and especially the old town, now a UNESCO World Heritage site, was not nearly as badly damaged.

The downtown area was full of Italians, you could hear my language everywhere. This was certainly in part because of the publicity Poland got in my country after the election of the Polish Pope to the Holy See in Rome two years ago. At the same time, not coincidentally, quite a few Poles managed to emigrate to Italy, legally or otherwise, to pick up jobs that Italians would not take, and they advertised their homeland in a way that other socialist countries just could not.

But the presence of aspiring Latin lovers also owed a lot to the reputation of Poland, together with other eastern European countries, as a place where one could easily trade a pair of stockings or jeans for a night of love. Well not love, really, just sex. I saw a few Italian families, some young couples, probably students, but very many single men, some quite old, on the prowl. I did not feel especially proud of my passport today.

The most fun part of the night was going back to the hotel in a horse-drawn carriage, entirely made of wood, that looked like it had just been plucked from a fairy tale. Well, in many ways we really were living through a fairy tale, thanks to our Polish friends, the organizational skills of Bogdan and a little (really, not much) hard currency in our wallets.

As we went to sleep, Andrew and I shared a room, Ann and Marzena another. It was great not to have to argue with hotel receptionists about whether we were students or foreigners. Marzena of course was neither, I wondered, but did not ask, how much they charged for her stay.

11 May 1980 – Krakow visit and the Moscow Olympics

Today we visited the city with Bogdan, who had hired a local tour guide to show us the sights. She was rather shy and underwhelming but we did learn a few bits and pieces of information as we went along.

Morning at the Wawel, an impressive castle that dated back to the very origin of the history of Poland as a country, in the X century. A few centuries later, during the Renaissance, it was developed to its grand appearance we could see today, in part thanks to Italian artists and architects. They came in large numbers because the beautiful lady Bona Sforza of Milan married King Sigismund I and influenced his decisions.

Excellent lunch at the restaurant of the Holiday Inn hotel. This was one of the few western chains that was allowed to operate in the country, clean hotel and upmarket restaurant. All meals for this trip were paid for by SGPiS, which was very kind of them! Afternoon touring downtown with Ann, we wanted to do some shopping but it was Sunday and most stores were closed.

During the afternoon I had only a start of a discussion with Pat, our classmate from New Jersey, who was in a particularly bad mood. Always a super-conservative, he was especially belligerent today. Only a start of a discussion because it was impossible to discuss with him, his thinking was too ideologically charged, so I let go. Despite his dislike for Democratic president Carter, whom he considered a spineless wimp, Pat supported his boycott of the Moscow Olympics in light of the Soviet invasion of Afghanistan.

I argued differently. I thought that politics and sports should always be kept separate. France had so decided and was sending its athletes to Moscow, and they would march under the French flag at the opening ceremony. Italy was sending its athletes but without a flag, only the seal of the Italian national olympic committee. I kind of agreed with my own country this time. Athletes should compete, but the national flag could stay home. Anyway I never liked that the Olympics became a competition among countries. I would rather have a competition among athletes. Or perhaps cities, like in ancient Greece. Pat would like to inflict infernal punishment on any American athlete who would want to attend the Olympics in Moscow.

Second great meal of the day in the hotel, then we all hit the sack early, it had been a long day.

12 May 1980 – Auschwitz

This was one of the most heart rending days of my life so far, and probably for a long time to come. We drove to the Nazi extermination camp of Auschwitz, in the nearby town of Oświęcim. Auschwitz was actually the germanized name of the Polish town.

The camp was now a museum and kept in pristine condition, and yet the atmosphere of death, the sinister smell and the vision of ghosts were all there, inescapable for me to feel, if not to see. The grotesquely sick irony of the gate sign: *Arbeit macht frei*, "work makes you free" set the tone for a sobering experience.

We visited the dormitories, large cold rectangular constructions with little more than wooden planks for beds. The execution wall still stood in its place, the sand underneath soaked in the blood of thousands of prisoners who were shot here. The crematorium with its ovens rebuilt after the war (the original ones had been destroyed by the Nazis when they fled and tried to hide the evidence of their crimes) was covered with fresh red flowers.

The most spine-chilling was the exhibition where artifacts were displayed: suitcases with the few belongings prisoners had been allowed to take from home, which were promptly confiscated upon arrival; each suitcase had the name of its owner written in white paint on the side, and his or her date of birth. One was marked *"Thomas Fischer, geboren 1941, klein Kind"* (Thomas Fischer, born in 1941, little child). What sick mind would care to note this information on a suitcase of a child who is about to be murdered? Answer: about 7,000 SS guards who shared the job of running Auschwitz until the arrival of Soviet troops in January 1945.

In another display, perhaps the most macabre, we could see lots of long female hair and samples of the cloth that was fabricated with it. Yet another displayed shoes, thousands of them. What for, for whom? What did they think when they piled them up this way? That someone was going to use them? Another grotesque display was full of thousands upon thousands of toothbrushes.

What happened at Auschwitz was obviously perpetrated by Nazi Germany but the western Allies of World War II also bear some responsibility. They knew about what was going on here, and did nothing. It was one Pole, Jan Karski, who later became one of our professors at Georgetown, who told the story as early as 1942, over two years before the liberation of the camp in January 1945. Karski had seen the mass extermination of Jews as it was taking place and reported back in report that made its way to London and Washington. He met British foreign minister Eden and even US president Roosevelt. They knew, they could have bombed the camp, or the railway lines carrying the prisoners, but did nothing.

We had a very late lunch at 16:30, we could just not get away from the museum, it was horrible and yet mesmerizing, we wanted to see it all. Including the sister concentration camp of Birkenau, where we were told even more people died than at the more famous Auschwitz. Altogether, some 1.1 million people died here, about 90% of them Jews, but also 150,000 Poles, 15,000 Gypsies, and 15,000 Soviet prisoners of war. Last year UNESCO elevated this camp to a World Heritage Site.[20]

I had to think about it, culture is not what first comes to mind at Auschwitz, but I understood that the need to preserve the memory of what happened here was a cultural necessity for the whole world. I wondered whether one day the same would be done with Soviet gulags, the camps set up by Stalin and some of which are still in operation in Siberia. Or with Mao's communist re-education camps in China. Or with the *Khmer Rouge*'s torture and extermination camps that were revealed to the world last year when Vietnam dislodged them from power. Or with the torture facilities still now in use by Latin American fascist military dictators. The UNESCO list of cultural horrors could become quite long indeed.

Afterwards a walk downtown to do a little shopping with Ann, but all stores closed at seven o'clock and we could not get much done. And we were not much in the mood for shopping anyway.

It had been an exhausting day, emotionally if not physically, and the evening was spent in the hotel room, reading and reflecting on the tragedy of the so called concentration camps, that were really extermination camps.

13 May 1980 – Salt mine and fine arts

Today we took a trip to yet another UNESCO World Heritage site of Poland, quite an unusual one this time: the salt mine in the town of Wielicka. A cranky lift lowered us about 80 meters into the earth's bowels and we then proceeded to walk around along the mine's shafts and tunnels. Not all 287 km of them, maybe just a couple, anyway

---

20 *I recommend reading the autobiographic book written by the commander of the camp, SS Rudolf Hoess, during his internment after the war, before he was executed for war crimes: "Death Dealer: the Memoir of the Commander of Auschwitz" with a foreword by Primo Levi, an Italian Jew who was imprisoned at Auschwitz but survived.*

long enough to have a pretty good idea of what it must feel like to work there.[21] The mine had been in operation for at least 700 years. Many sculptures adorned its walls, including a "last supper" low relief carved on the black salt after Leonardo's famous painting displayed in Milan. Of course, in catholic Poland there was also a chapel.

As we visited the mine, Pat picked up a cute blond girl from East Germany and started to chat away. Two girls in fact. They seemed quite available to socialize. More so than most people we met in East Germany itself. Good luck to him, I thought, maybe they would mellow him out a bit.

By the afternoon we were back in Krakow, and went to visit the Museum of Fine Arts and the Czartorysky collection. Again lots of Italian art, which made me feel proud in a way that my cheap-sex-hunting compatriots had not.

The highlight of the museum was a painting of the *Madonna with an ermine* by Leonardo da Vinci. He completed it at the Sforza castle in Milan in the 1480s or 1490s. The lady was probably Cecilia Gallerani, a beautiful woman Leonardo had met while there. We had seen earlier the ties that bound the Sforza family to Krakow since Bona had married Sigismund I. The painting got lost in the following centuries until it resurfaced again here in this city in 1800, brought back by the wealthy madame Isabela Czartorysky. It then popped up in France in 1830, before returning to Poland in 1876. During World War II it was looted by the Germans and slightly damaged, but it was later restored and returned.

I reflected how I did not understand my compatriots when they complained about too much Italian art having found its way to foreign owners and museums. As long as it was well preserved and easily accessible it was good publicity for the country. In fact quite often our masterpieces were better taken care of abroad than in Italy. Of course, much Italian art was stolen, which can never be accepted, and it was then not easily accessible to the public, but rather hidden away in private collections, which is even less acceptable, but that is another story.

---

21 *Commercial salt mining would be discontinued in 1996 as it had become economically unprofitable for a long time but the mine continued to be a major tourist attraction of historical interest.*

14 May 1980 – Pieskowa Skala

We spent the morning walking around town for some shopping, but as usual quantity and quality left a lot to be desired. Nevertheless I did find something quite interesting: an old Atlas, a huge book printed in Germany right after World War I, which still showed the old German Empire, when Poland, carved up by Russia, Germany and Austria, did not exist as a country.

The map of Germany shows the then new, post World War I, borders, but also, in dotted lines, it nostalgically marked the old borders of the Reich. It took many Germans a long time to accept the territorial losses after that war, for starting which they had been blamed beyond their share of responsibility by the Treaty of Versailles. Funny to find this imperial German atlas here. Polish-German relations have always been touchy, to put it mildly. They were terrible in the first half of the XX century. A great buy for 2500 złoty.

Bogdan warned me I might have problems taking it out of the country, because anything produced before 1945 was considered part of the national patrimony and could not be exported except with a special permission. Why 1945? Why not Polish independence after World War I? Again a question to which it would be futile to look for an answer. I thought I would take a chance, part with my 2500 złoty and see what happened with the exportation. Perhaps I could try some *kombinować*. Anyway I did not feel very guilty about taking a German book which showed maps of Europe without Poland out of the country.

In the afternoon we drove to the *Pieskowa Skała* (the Rock of the Little Dog) castle. Quite impressive construction. Again I was proud to see some of Italian art. Apparently the queen of Poland at the time came from the Florentine Medici family and tried to take as much as possible from her native Tuscany to decorate her new home.

Not much here was Polish. Not much was here at all really. To make up for the dearth of exhibits they even displayed pictures of objects which were at other museums elsewhere in Poland. The whole place was a bit run down. We had to wear some funny slippers to preserve the tired parquet, I could not really see the point but I guessed it was just as good to try and preserve the preservable and hope for some well funded restoration sometime soon.

15 May 1980 – Dunajec cruise and promises of liberation

Today we had a totally different kind of experience. A day trip to the Dunajec river, on the border with Czechoslovakia. We drifted down the river for some 18 km on a big wooden raft piloted by some quite deft local sailors over a brisk current and even some small rapids. It was very cold and windy for mid-May. We were all cuddled up in our coats and hoods, trying to peek out enough to enjoy the breathtaking mountain scenery.

We stopped for lunch at a local eatery along the banks of the river, 100 złoty for a hearty meal of sausages and potatoes with a hot soup on the side. Cheap, tasty and filling. And warming, most importantly. True Polish countryside cuisine.

During the boat ride, we often got very close to the Czechoslovak bank, and a few local people from the villages along the river come down here and there to have a look at us. Some waved and smiled in our direction, as people the world over when they see boats sail by.

The Czechoslovak regime was far harsher on its own people than the Polish one. It made it harder for them to travel abroad, to have any contact with foreigners, to receive information from independent sources. Czechoslovakia had tried, of course, the path to "socialism with a human face" in 1968, when Communist leader Dubcek experimented with a much more tolerant version of one-party rule. The result was an intervention of armies from the "socialist brother countries" to save the proletariat revolution from reactionary forces that wanted to restore capitalism. Translation: the USSR decided that Dubcek had gone too far and cracked down, forcing other Warsaw Pact countries to chip in their fair share of tanks to make it look like a collective action.

Only fiercely independent Romania, under dictator Ceausescu, had refused to participate: not that he wanted to defend Dubcek's liberal approach. To the contrary, Ceausescu was the most brutal of all Communist dictators in Europe. But he wanted to protect the principle that each country should have its own approach to socialism as long as it did not openly challenge Soviet hegemony. Invading Czechoslovakia established a precedent and Ceausescu feared Romania might have been next if it strayed too much from Soviet orthodoxy. Since then, under new chief Husak, Czechoslovakia had become a stalwart fortress of near stalinist politics and economics.

It was very embarrassing to hear Pat stand up on our raft and yell at the hapless Czechoslovaks from the top of his lungs: "Hang in there, we'll come to liberate you from Communism!". Once, twice, three times... If only... He thought he was being funny, or perhaps we really believed it but I thought it was irresponsible. It was also embarrassing with Bogdan and Marzena on the boat with us.

People in this part of the world had memories of such promises in the past, when it was western (especially American) government agencies, such as Voice of America, that gave false illusions to the peoples oppressed by the USSR. Especially when Hungary rose in 1956, many brave Hungarians actually believed that NATO could come forward and liberate them. But it did not, and they were crushed by Soviet tanks.

In the evening we were back in Krakow. Good dinner in a local restaurant, as almost always, lots of meat and potatoes. Andrew and I took a walk to the Wawel, hoping to catch a night view, but it was closed and watched by threatening dogs, so we turned around and ended the evening with a chat in the cool wind.

16 May 1980 – Zakopane and *Juwenalia*

Another day trip, this time to Zakopane, a ski resort in the Tatra mountains, next to the border with Czechoslovakia. It was still unseasonably cold for May. We took a nice and easy walking tour of the town. It would be much better to come here in full winter, for skiing, or in summer, for hiking the breathtaking mountains. Now we could not do either! Still, it was quite pleasant to soak in the scenery, the atmosphere of the town, in good company and in front of substantial Polish food and drinks served to us for lunch at a simple local eatery.

In one quaint shop I bought a tea set: pot, six cups, and a milk jar for 2500 złoty, nice souvenir.

Dinner in the early evening at the *Staropolska*. Our local guide, Halska, insisted this was a "typical" restaurant, but I hoped she was wrong. It was really nothing special, a smoky joint with mediocre, stale and dry food.

Today it was the start of the *Juwenalia*, a kind of annual nation-wide youth celebration during which college students go around town asking for money. Seemed like a Halloween for older kids. They made more noise than children and asked for money instead of candies.

17 May 1980 – Back to Warsaw, meet Cathy

In the morning I took another tour of the city on foot with Ann. *Juwenalia* was still ongoing, but somehow it was not so sparkling as we had been led to anticipate. The students just did not seem excited and were not so exciting. Most walked around aimlessly trying with no conviction to get money from passersby. It looked like they were just going through the motions, who knows why. It was not a politically colored event, not apparently anyway, but it felt like one.

At 3:00pm departure back to Warsaw, but this time by plane. It was a Soviet-made aircraft operated by LOT, the national flag carrier of Poland. The plane itself was quite spartan and noisy. Service aboard was basic, to put it mildly.

There was a smoking section of the cabin and a non-smoking one, but the funny thing was that they were not positioned, respectively, in the back and in the front of the cabin, like in the aircraft of most airlines. Here, and in all eastern European airlines, smokers and non-smokers were assigned to the left and right of the aisle. The latter of course provided no shielding whatsoever to the cigarette exhausts, with the obvious result that all non-smokers received generous wafts of smoke no matter where they were seated.

I was never able to understand why the designers of the cabin made this choice, it was so disarmingly silly. Maybe it was made so as not to favor anyone: in the normal cabin layout those in the non-smoking section, but close to the smoking rows, were penalized compared to those who sat away from them.

On western planes usually I tried to get a seat as far forward in the cabin so as to be away from the smokers, except that if you are too far forward and it is a small aircraft you end up just behind the smokers of the business class. On this plane everyone was on the same level and had an equal chance to enjoy passive smoking and get their clothes stinky at destination. I suppose it was a more egalitarian approach.

The upside (for us) of the flight was that it cost us just 7 dollars per person: obviously the airline, like so many other state-owned businesses in Poland, was flying at a loss!

Once back in Warsaw we met Cathy, Ann's friend who would be traveling with us for the rest of our stay in eastern Europe and then back to Italy. She had just flown in from the United States and was a bit jet-lagged but otherwise in good spirits and excited for the experience ahead of us.

In the evening we went for dinner at Marian and Ewa's, where I met Angela, the wife of my cousin Niccolò, a surgeon who came to Poland for a medical conference. They were new to Poland and asked lots of questions, and Ewa and Marian proved to be, as always, a source of prolific if unorthodox information.

18 May 1980 – More phone calls, customs controls, newspapers and cars

Around noon I asked Ann to help me make a phone call to the medical center in Gdansk where my cousin was attending a conference so we could coordinate to meet when he came to Warsaw. We went to a payphone around the school for which we needed change, and I had come equipped with a small pile of coins. Unfortunately Ann dialed the wrong number and before we knew the devilish machine had gobbled up half our coins. We could not find anyone to change some paper money into coins so we were stuck.

Then Ann noted that her friend Ewa (yes, a pretty common name in Poland) was setting up a stand to sell *pączki-sernik* to make money for the *Akademyk,* a student association she belonged to. These are a kind of golf-ball shaped cheesecakes that usually contain some vodka in the egg and cheese mix, they say the reason is it makes the cake absorb less fat. They were quite cheap so I bought half the stock just to get change. It was all pretty funny but I got the change, Ann made the call, Ewa was almost sold out even before she had set up her stand and we all ate *pączki–sernik*, which by the way were quite tasty!

Today I witnessed some creative trading with Angela. You could buy some luxury goods very cheap here, in black market dollars, that is. Like fur: mink, fox, ... And an Italian lady would not let that opportunity pass would she? But buying the fur coat was the easy part. Taking it (and one or two more for girlfriends) out of the country would be much more challenging, since of course luxury goods bought in the free market with hard currency, and no official receipts, could not legally be exported.

But Marian knew someone who knew someone else who worked at the airport customs control. For 100 dollars in cash they were willing to close an eye on her departing luggage.

The way it worked was that on the day of departure, after check-in and passport control, ALL luggage, including big suitcases that would go into the hold of the aircraft, were visually inspected by customs officials. Almost all passengers (except some diplomats or lucky ones when the airport got busy and there were not enough inspectors) would have to place their suitcases on a bench and open them for the guards to look and stick their hands inside, move things around, unpack and repack if they so chose.

They were looking for stuff that was cheap locally, either because it was produced in Poland, but not sold through the legal commercial channels; or because it was coming from other socialist countries (mostly the USSR) at subsidized prices. Caviar was a prime example, but also furs, carpets from Central Asia, and gold. It was entirely up to the customs official to pick which bags to check and how thoroughly. They could not open and inspect every single one of the departing suitcases, especially on a busy day, so inevitably it became a random check. Or not so random... If she or he was willing to close an eye, the departing passenger could get away with anything. Today Angela cruised though customs with her furs, no problems at all.

In the afternoon I went to the post office and tried to call Ben, my former roommate at Georgetown, to sort out where to store for the upcoming summer the stuff I had left behind in a hurry to come to Poland. After a long wait at the post office, over an hour and a half, I had to give up, despite the fact I had booked my very own time slot for an international phone call.

While killing time I tried to buy a newspaper. Foreign papers had wildly different prices: *Pravda* (meaning "truth" in Russian) the official paper of the Communist Party of the USSR, cost only 20 groszy (cents of złoty), practically nothing, subsidized propaganda. The Italian Communist party's paper, *l'Unità*, cost 5 złoty, ie 25 times more, but heck it was still communist prose. *La Stampa* cost 32 złoty, 160 times more than *Pravda*: with two daily papers' worth you would spend the equivalent of a whole year of "Truth". Perhaps because it was owned by the capitalist billionaires of the Italian Agnelli family, the friends of Poland who had invested in building cheap FIAT cars here. Anyway I bought *La Stampa*, I needed some updates of what was happening in the world. The paper was a few days old but better than nothing.

19 May 1980 – Soviet visa and another duck

In the morning we drove to the Soviet consulate to pick up our visas. We knew comrade Leonid Brezhnev, the President of the USSR and General Secretary of the Communist Party of the Soviet Union was on an official visit to Poland for the celebrations of the 25th anniversary of the foundation of the Warsaw Pact and I joked he should pop in to make sure our visas were ready. Of all people, who did we see driving past us as we approached the imposing building? Yes, Brezhnev, no less! He sat, as per protocol, in the rear right-hand seat of a big black armored car and we recognized him without a shadow of a doubt through the thick darkened glass of the official car thanks to his distinctive thick eyebrows implanted on his stone face.

Relations between Poland and the USSR were a bit tense at that time. Moscow did not like Poland's relatively freestyle communism. The Polish brother party allowed lots of easy contacts between the people and the West and enforced little ideological discipline, never mind the large room for maneuver enjoyed by the Catholic Church, especially after the election in 1978 of pope John Paul II, the erstwhile bishop of Krakow, and his triumphal visit to his home country last year. In a year of rising East-West tensions over Afghanistan, human rights and American rapprochement with China, the imminent deployment of new US nuclear missiles in Europe in response to Soviet missiles, etc. this was not good news for the USSR as it tried to close the ranks of the Warsaw Pact.

Our visas were ready and were quickly handed over by a dour employee of the embassy. Unlike most visas issued by countries the world over, it was not stamped on our passport, but rather it was a separate pink piece of paper, with all of our data in Cyrillic alphabet, the precise itinerary we were booked for, and a photograph. All of which would be taken away from us at the end of our journey in the USSR. Andrew speculated that they did not wanted the sacred seal of the USSR to be circulating freely and fall into the wrong hands somewhere in the capitalist world!

Luckily, I took a picture of it as a souvenir. It stipulated exactly where and when we were allowed to go in the USSR. For every day we had prepaid our accommodation to *Intourist*, the Soviet tourism board. We could not change dates, itinerary, hotel/camping site or means of transportation: Giallina's plate number was also registered and we had to be with her throughout our stay.

Then it was the turn of the local police station to renew our visas where Andrew noticed his wallet was missing. He was quite worried and went to book a phone call to his parents in the States at the post office, he wanted to cancel his credit card and have some money sent to him. As we were leaving to go to eat, a young couple encountered us in the steps with Andrew's wallet. Andrew was luckier than I was in Vienna. He therefore dropped in the post office to cancel his call home and we just happened to station Giallina in a No Standing Zone. A policeman came up, asked a few questions, wanted to know how we could be students if we did not speak Polish, and finally concluded: "Well, I can't fine students".

It seemed that in this trip we were making a habit out of getting in trouble with law enforcement officials and then get away with it.

In the afternoon the three of us went for a round of shopping, we wanted to find some porcelain to take home but could not find anything of quality worth buying. Prices were reasonable for us but a proper set of tea cups and pot would cost an average Pole some half of his monthly salary. At least the official salary, but as we knew well by now very little here was official, and very much was *kombinować*, the art of solving problems circumventing the (often illogical) law.

In the evening dinner at our "first duck place", where we had eaten one of our first meals when we arrived in Warsaw last February for this incredible experience which is about to come to a close. We called it "the first duck place" to distinguish it from the "second duck place" we found a few days later. Good duck at cheap (for us) prices. I never had much duck before in my life, maybe never had it at all come to think of it. Chicken, turkey, quail, even pheasant but not duck. We tried to ask around why duck was such a popular dish in Poland but could not really find an answer. Anyway I now liked it quite a bit and I would make sure I would have it every now and then when back home in Italy. Or back home at Georgetown, in the United States.

Home? What was my "home"? Where was it? Sometimes I thought about it while driving around Poland. I was Italian, but had lived in the States for a few years, and now felt more and more comfortable in Poland, at home in Warsaw really. I liked that feeling: to feel at home where I was at any given time. Maybe I had just been lucky, I thought, to have spent time in hospitable places and made good friends? Maybe I was a nomad by nature?

I reflected that I was too young to deliver a verdict yet. Too young to have developed roots anywhere. And anyway somehow I had the feeling I did not like having roots. I saw them as a limitation rather than as an asset. Surely my inclination would evolve with age. For now I was sure that I preferred to have wings rather than roots, and travel the world and absorb different values and cultures. I would have more time to make up my mind later in life.

20 May 1980 – UNESCO, engine oil and Russia's future

Funny episode today. I went for a walk to the *Stare Miasto* (Old City), which some Poles told me they expect to become a UNESCO World heritage Site later this year.[22]

After parking I was approached by one of the usual illegal parking "guardians" who promised to look after my car for a tip. Same as in Rome, really. But perhaps more useful here, where petty theft of windshield wipers and light bulbs was apparently a much more common occurrence. In fact when you walked around you saw most cars which were parked in the street had their windshield wipers removed to prevent them from being stolen. They would be very difficult to replace, not so much for the cost, but because of unpredictable availability of supplies.

The "Five-year Plan", that Leninist invention whereby the state decides what is to be produced by the country's factories, does not work: what is produced is often not needed, and what is needed is not produced. No planning authority can make up demand and supply.

Anyway, after agreeing on a tip we chatted a bit. He did not speak any English so our only common language, beyond my basic

---

22 *The old city would indeed receive the title in September 1980.*

Polish, was German. I used my German quite often during this trip, beginning with the day we were arrested at the Warsaw Pact military base in Czechoslovakia. Many Poles spoke German, not as many as spoke English or Russian (which was compulsory in school) perhaps but more than spoke French or any other language. Generally speaking, Poles were pretty good with foreign languages. I had only studied German for a year and a half at Georgetown, but practice makes perfect, and I was pleased my German was useful and improving.

He told me of his detention in German camps as a prisoner of war in 1944, where he learned the language. A grim experience but somehow he managed to survive it and now it turned out to be useful for him to speak German, he could talk to tourists.

He asked how much it would cost to buy a car in Italy. Because he did not understand Italian lire, he asked how many months' salary an average worker would have to devote to the purchase.

- Well, it depends – I said – what kind of car?
- Let's say a *Polonez* – he replied. (A *Polonez* was a FIAT model produced in Poland on the chassis of the FIAT 125, a mass produced family vehicle, reliable and affordable if rather unsightly, despite having been designed by renowned Giorgetto Giugiaro.)
- Not many people would really bother to buy a *Polonez* in Italy – I responded, and he was not a little disappointed – but if they did it might cost some 4-5 months' wages to an average worker.
– Really? – he replied with eyes wide open – Pretty good, here it would cost about eight years of wages, 400,000 złotys.

It was hard to calculate the cost of a car in this way, the purchasing power of the złoty could not really be compared with that of a convertible currency, even a weak one like the Italian lira. But anyway I got the point.

He then started to share his views on world history, past and future. He believed the first great empire in history was Rome, and the second that of Bismarck's Germany. The third one would be Russia's new empire, not the one of the Tsars but the current version. Russia was economically weak today, but had great potential and would rise to rule the world. It must be that way, there was no other possibility, he emphasized with conviction.

He did not sound like he was an indoctrinated communist and did not say once he hoped for socialism to prevail under the leadership of the Soviet Union. In fact he did not even mention the Soviet Union at all, or socialism for that matter.

He spoke of Russia as the nation that was somehow destined to lead the world in the next century. I was not sure whether I should have been more amused or worried, but I did not take the conversation much further, because of both language limitations and lack of a meaningful exchange. But it was interesting to listen to him for a short while.

He was very helpful: I had a problem with the lubricant oil of Giallina's engine and he helped sort it out, for which he got a nice tip. One of those nice people you meet along the way of life, share an intense moment with, shake hands and never meet again.

After my walk about the old city I caught up with Ann, Cathy and Andrew and we went to the Czechoslovak consulate to apply for another transit visa, we would need it to drive back to Italy at the end of our stay next month. I also asked for a map of the country, I surely wanted to avoid getting arrested again at a military base, but none was available. We would have to keep our eyes open and hope for the best.

21 May 1980 – Another visa, food and dreams

Quick trip to the consulate of the Hungarian People's Republic for yet another visa, which we would need as we decided we would transit through that country, instead of Austria, on our way back to Italy. Ann, Andrew and I, as "locals" (because we were somehow officially categorized as "permanent" students here though we were only temporary ones) paid only 160 złoty, but Cathy, who was just a visitor, had to pay in dollars: six dollars to be precise, hardly breaking the bank but they wanted hard currency from the western capitalist visitor. Our status as students had brought several advantages over the last months, in favorable rates at hotels for example. But sadly no right to buy gasoline for our car at the local price.

Today we managed to fix a problem with Giallina's accelerator. The wire connecting the pedal to the ignition had snapped. Went to a first mechanic who could not really fix it but managed to tie it up so we could drive, but only in first gear. Better than nothing. We then drove, very slowly, to another mechanic who put our little car back in full working order. This proved this VW designed almost half a century ago was not the cutting edge of technology any more but was simple enough for almost any mechanic to put his hands on and repair.

After which we all went for yet another great dinner at Marzena's. I just could not get used to this, it was just too much. All this great food on the table and yet there was always a bit of a sad atmosphere during these meals, despite our by now deep friendship with her family and mutual trust. She, and everyone else in the family, rarely smiled.

Marzena's father joined us today, he had a day off work. He was a pilot, and had served in the Polish air force, but had retired from active service and for a few years now had been flying small planes to spray crops over large fields in the countryside near Warsaw. He was quite fit for his age. He was a serious person, did not speak much, but seemed to be always in a good mood.

Her brother Marek was a cool guy, handsome and soft spoken. He did not speak much either but he, too, dreamed of a free life in the West. In fact our conversations at these meals were a bit repetitive when it came to this. Our gracious Polish host did not relent in their uninterrupted litany of complaints about, well, Poland. We fully understood them of course, and mostly agreed with them. It was just that I personally felt a bit frustrated in hearing the same stories over and over again when I could do very little of any use.

Actually, eventually I thought that maybe there was something I could do. Marzena wanted to visit me in Italy, and I would do my best to fulfill her wish. This just might open the door for her (and perhaps the rest of the family?) to move to a better life in western Europe or America.

Yet it was a little depressing to think that their problems were the same for virtually all other Poles we met in the last three months. There were millions of people whose energies were restrained by the straight-jacket of real socialism. To change that, Poles themselves would have to take their destiny in their own hands. Hard to imagine given current geopolitics but history is dotted with stuff that was considered unimaginable until, when no one expected, it happened.

22 May 1980 – Drive to Gniew and rock music in Gdansk

Today we had planned to drive to Gdansk, known as Danzig when it was German, in the north of the country, by its Baltic Sea shores. Of course, we could not leave without our by now almost-daily meal at Marzena's. We had a fun conversation to start off the day and were served a sumptuous breakfast, lots of proteins and caffeine. Today it was a truly superlative menu: scrambled eggs, bacon bits, hard boiled eggs, sweet cheese, hard cheese, dark Polish bread, butter, jam, cucumbers, even fresh and really red tomatoes! Good, we would appreciate the nourishment during our long drive later today.

Where they could find the stuff was going to remain a mystery. Maybe her father, with his connections to the armed forces, had his secret supply channels, though he did not seem that kind of guy. We did not ask.

After cleaning Giallina ourselves in a parking lot (somehow today we could not find the usual cleaners who do it for a couple of dollars) we set off northward, on a road along the Vistula.

From the road we saw the skyline of the town of Płock on the right bank of the Vistula, but decided to skip it to save time. We did drive into the next town, Włocławek, but got out of it as quickly as possible because it was very polluted. Driving along a winding and altogether pleasant road we enjoyed the rolling landscape along the river. No time for much sightseeing though, we had to reach Gdansk tonight.

The only city we visited in some detail was charming Toruń. It was entirely Gothic, including a Town Hall smack in the middle of the *rynek starego miasta*, the picturesque old market square. The heart of the city, like in many Polish towns, was built during the Renaissance.

We negotiated our way out of Toruń through some winding side roads. Just after Toruń we pulled up at a road-side eatery to stop out stomachs rumbling. What was wrong with us? After the huge morning breakfast at Marzena's we had stored enough calories for a week, we should not be hungry! We were quite lucky as today they had freshly picked mushrooms from the nearby forest on the menu. Stir-fried and very savory. Mushrooms were some of the best staple food we had in Poland, and they paired amazingly well with the ubiquitous ducks.

After lunch we chose to continue on secondary country roads instead of the highway. We all agreed it would be more interesting, you never knew whom you might meet. We were in Pomerania, a land of ancient Teutonic (German really) roots and deep historical significance because of that. The mix of Polish and German culture, from the names of the location to the architecture, was inescapable.

Once out in the country I, not normally a flower person, for some reason thought of stopping the car so we could all go out in the field and pick dandelions. A bee chased us back to the car but luckily we escaped unhurt.

We did take a little time off at Gniew, the Polish name for the old Mewe fort of the Teutonic Knights, it was a really fascinating sight and, even though we did not have time to explore it in detail, we decided to drive into the old town: it was then that I read in my guidebook that the most interesting sight of the town was... the view from the road!

Then another quick pit stop to buy some gasoline. Even though we did not know the guy at the service station he saw our foreign plate and immediately proposed a deal for some fuel at slightly more than local Polish price.

We finally arrived in Gdansk at sunset, after some 450km of driving, and found two rooms at the hotel Monopol. We were exhausted after a long day and decided we would have dinner there, just eat and relax, and go to bed early.

If only... Little did we know, there was a very loud, unbearable cacophony emanating from a nearby locale where a rock group played thoroughly bone-shattering music (hard to think of it as music, more like noise, really) until midnight. Yet the locals seemed to appreciate it, there were lots of people in attendance shaking and swinging on the dance floor lit with psychedelic strobe lights. Our sleep would have to wait until they all exhausted their considerable energy.

It seemed that, even though Poland did have access to most western music, there was still a fairly naive attitude to rock and roll: the louder the better. Not unlike what one could find in smaller Italian provincial towns, only more so. Rock music as an act of protest was a thing of the past in the West by 1980, but I had a feeling it was still very much a thing of the present here in Poland.

Or maybe, at the ripe age of twenty, I was just getting old ahead of time and could no longer, well, resonate with this kind of stuff.

23 May 1980 – Gdansk money, old atlas and music

It got a bit complicated at the hotel in the morning when we came down for breakfast because Cathy was considered a "visitor" while we three were "locals" because we were full-time students. Therefore, the receptionist asked her to pay in hard currency, exchanged at the official rack rate, while we could pay a much lower rate, in złoty. The difference was huge, about four times the cost of the room in black market money. And we had to stay at least two nights. After a quick round of consultations the four of us decided to pay up for the first night and then check her out. Then Ann, Andrew and I would check-in again as locals and we would pretend she was gone. She would sneak back into the hotel tonight unofficially, into one of the rooms we would rent in our names, as students.

The hotel guy looked at us and, although he could not understand English, he surely figured that out: obviously we would not let Cathy sleep in the car for the second night, but he did not really care. As long as we did not get him in trouble with the authorities for renting a room at Polish prices to a foreign visitor he was willing to close an eye. The hotel was obviously state-owned, so for him it was better to get no money at all from Cathy than to get the Polish rate that could get him in trouble.

We spent the whole day touring the major sights of Gdansk, especially the romantic *Śródmieście* (historical downtown). The Artus Court, a medieval market and social meeting place was part of the new museum, with a charming XVII century bronze statue of a naked Neptune at the entrance.[23]

The town hall was an impressive example of late Gothic architecture. This was a city soaked in history. It was here that, for Europeans anyway, World War II began with the German attack on Westerplatte, as our landlady in Berlin had so vividly narrated to us. (From a more global viewpoint, and it was a "World" war after all, it

---

23 *During a later restoration in 1988 a fig leaf was applied to cover the genitals of Neptune, who must have wondered what he did wrong to deserve this after almost four centuries of faithful service to the city. I guess this was an idea coming from the Church, who was gaining influence at the time.*

began with the Japanese invasion of China at least two years earlier.) Virtually no one disputed that Gdansk was in Poland to stay, but the character of the city clearly showed a partly Germanic identity that no treaty could ever erase.

We needed more Polish currency and tried some street changers, many of whom were available at every corner of the downtown area, but unsuccessfully. They all tried to rip us off. I was thinking, could you theoretically cheat someone who is trying to illegally change money with unauthorized currency dealers at black market rates? Cheating the cheaters? Anyway, their technique was always the same: they first accepted any exchange rate we suggested, and handed us the złoty equivalent, minus 50 or 100 złoty. When we counted the money and pointed out that they were short-changing us, they started arguing and tried to take our hard currency away from our hands. We were alert enough to avoid having our bank notes grabbed, at which point they wanted their złotys back and ran away, to try their luck with some other tourist.

At a second-hand bookstore I found another beautiful atlas, printed in 1923, which I bought for 1000 złoty. The bookseller warned me that I might have problems exporting it because it was made before 1945, it was considered a national treasure etc. all stuff I already knew but it was a beautiful book and I decided to take a chance. We would see, I was sure Marian could help. Polish second-hand bookstores could be real treasure troves for a bibliophile.

In the evening we attended a classical concert. The Gdansk Philharmonic played a program of Brahms (violin concerto) and Sibelius (2nd symphony). They played quite well in my opinion, but the concert hall was very much beat up. Tired furniture and chairs, faded colors. It could have used an energetic facelift. However, I must say that this period of time in Poland has offered many excellent opportunities to listen to excellent classical music players. At very reasonable prices, at least for us.

Dinner at the *Pod Lososiem* (Under the salmon) restaurant, where I tasted a juicy and tender piece of liver. The others had, more appropriately than me, grilled salmon steaks, or perch, which were also quite tasty. I did not know they produced salmon in Poland, though apparently some farms had managed to thrive inland thanks to sources of appropriate water.[24]

---

24 *In 2018 still there at Szeroka 52/54, 22-100 Gdańsk, Poland.*

I wondered, but forgot to ask a native speaker, why so many restaurants in Poland were named "Under *something*" where *something* was some kind of animal: pigeon, dove, crocodile and now a salmon. There must be a reason, I am not sure that is done anywhere else in the world.

After a long day of visiting, we deserved a good night sleep and dreamed of some warm weather for the coming days.

24 May 1980 – To Hel (one L) and back

It was certainly a cold day in Hel today! We got up insanely early in the cold morning to board a small ferry to the town of Hel (one "L") on the eponymous peninsula. Nothing special to see or do. Lots of strange stray dogs with no tail were roaming around, and the landscape was decorated with tons of dead fish on the beach. Strong winds and drizzling rain completed a bizarre environment into which we set our *wanderlust* free.

A kind of cold hell (two "L") you might say? It all made for a perplexing scenery. This was supposed to be a much sought-after seaside resort but the weather was not encouraging now, it was very cold, no one was around, perhaps tourists would materialize later in the season, I guessed we were just a couple of months too early.

From Hel we took another slow boat to Sopot, a nice little resort/spa town. Long walks until we stopped for some Baltic cod and chips and a beer on the terrace of a simple restaurant (60 złoty). In the meantime the sun had briefly graced us with its appearance in the sky, which put us all in a better mood.

We almost missed the boat to go back to Gdansk in the evening, as a sea gale (force 6, they told us) caused the cancellation of several ferry rides. Curiously, we had to buy a ticket to gain access to the ticket office, surely a first in our lives and probably the last time we would have such a unique opportunity. They explained to us this was because the peer where the ticket office was located was considered a special public "garden", and the receipts from the tickets contributed to its maintenance. Really strange but well, we got both sets of tickets.

Again we unsuccessfully tried to change some money on the black market but the changers' technique was always the same so that by the end of the day we could not conclude a clean, honest and transparent black market currency transaction!

It had been a long day, but we grabbed some food somewhere. It was so not memorable I forgot to write about it. After which we went back to our hotel and smoothly smuggled Cathy in so she would not have to pay the crazy tourist rack rate. We all felt tired and a bit cold, and hit the sack without the usual card games or chat and comments that regularly characterized our unwinding at the end of each day.

25 May 1980 – Gdansk to Oliwa and the Masurian lakes

Late departure after a leisurely and abundant breakfast that did not end before 10:30, but we forgave ourselves as yesterday had been a long day... Had to smuggle Cathy out the same way we had smuggled her in, as officially she never spent a night at the hotel. Anyway we finally got going and headed for Oliwa, a suburb of Gdansk with an interesting abbey that exuded history from every brick. This was a major headquarters for the Cistercian monks for centuries. Poland's catholic roots reached quite deep back into the past indeed. It was also a proud town, even an independent city-state when it was briefly separated from the city state of Free Gdansk in the 1920s. A huge organ adorned the church but sadly no one was playing.

We then moved toward Malbork, where we arrived in the late morning to admire the imposing fortress. Our next stop was the Masurian region. Finally we got some sunny weather and could fully enjoy the luxuriant countryside. The small towns and villages we drove through were rather desolate however, much poorer than those we had seen in the south of the country.

We reached Olsztyn at dinner time and ended up eating at the Karolowe (chez Charles) restaurant. We had no clue where to go and this was a recommendation from a slightly out-of-date guidebook from the Italian Touring Club I had with me. We gobbled up a less than impressive meal but it was filling and really cheap.

After the early dinner we decided we were sufficiently unimpressed and therefore would leave Olsztyn behind, drive on and try to find a place to sleep at the next town, Ruciane Nida. Not that we had any reason to believe Ruciane Nida would be more impressive than Olsztyn, but we just felt like driving on.

In the meantime we needed fuel for Giallina. We found a station and bought 48 liters. The man at the pump agreed to sell us fuel at the Polish price but, curiously, refused to take his cut like all his other colleagues we had ever dealt with. When I asked him why he did not want his "commission" for allowing us to buy without the required coupons for foreigners, he replied too quickly for me to fully understand but Ann told us he said something along the lines of "this is the right price for Poles and it should be the same for foreigners, screw the government rules". He was a really honest black market fuel seller.

When we reached Ruciane Nida there was no hotel to speak of, so we decided to move on to Wygryny, a small village of a few hundred people. We stopped and asked some passersby for directions to a hotel, any hotel, and they looked at us with puzzled expressions that I interpreted as meaning: "Where are you trying to go this late in the evening in this god-forsaken neck of the wood?" Anyway they had no recommendations for any place for us to sleep. Slightly worried, as it was getting late, we drove on and ran into a bunch of drunks staggering along the sidewalk who could not believe they got free entertainment making fun of us fools.

Then luck seemed about to strike when a tiny old man we stopped told us he was building a hotel. Unfortunately he hastened to add that it would not be ready to open its doors for business before sometime next year! However, a big signpost from the PTTK (the Polish Tourist Board) announced that "the trees are our friends". Which was just as well as it looked like we might have to spend the night with their sole protection over our heads.

At this point we had nothing to lose so we fearlessly drove on and reached Pisz, a small town of some 20,000 souls. It was past 10pm but we found a small hotel with two rooms. We even managed to smuggle Cathy in as a student of SGPiS so that she could pay the reduced rate like the three of us.

The evening ended with the four of us sharing a few beers and playing cards, after which Andrew and Cathy went to sleep. Ann and I played our usual *scopa* card game into the night. She finally caught on that I had been cheating for weeks using my uncle Zio Gigi's tricks. Oh well, I would now have to play honestly. Ann and I stayed up for a long conversation under the crystal clear sky, with a full moon warmly watching from above and a myriad bright stars sparkling brightly all around us.

26 May 1980 – Rowing in the wind

There was a pretty lake near Pisz and we wanted to rent a canoe or a row-boat. We saw many boats lying on the banks of the lake and asked around but no chance, a couple of rental shops said all their boats were reserved. There was no one around, the place was clearly not busy. Not one single boat was in the water. I suggested to Ann that she try her best Polish, put on a nice smile, discretely waggle some dollar banknotes and then repeat our request. She did and, magically, we could choose any boat we wanted! Probably the boat rentals were state owned, and the employees knew that their salary would not change whether they rented the boats out or not. But a fistful of dollars (7 dollars for 4 hours to be precise) in their pocket would obviously make a difference.

This made me think about how deeply rooted corruption was in this country. I was not even sure it was appropriate to call it corruption. Corruption means you are doing something wrong, out of line, disruptive of the system, for personal advantage. But here it was a way of life, it was normal, it was expected and universally practiced. It was not against the system, it was the system, it was a way, sometimes the only way, to get things done, big and small. It was absolutely necessary to break free of the straitjacket of the planned economy.

After handing over the seven greenback bills we chose a boat and rowed out into the lake. The sky was cloudy but it did not rain and it was altogether pleasant. It was cool and windy but fun to be out in the water and do some exercise.

After a while, it got really cool and really windy and it was difficult to steer our boat back to the peer we started from. The man who rented the boat to us saw this and come out to tow us back with a small outboard. It felt a bit humiliating, especially as we were never really in danger, but still, it was helpful! We gave him three dollars as an extra tip for getting us out of trouble and he was so happy that as we left we saw him literally jumping around with joy.

27 May 1980 – Getting lost in the Masurian lakes region

After breakfast we got through the usual issues at checkout: they needed an exchange receipt and we argued we were students. We got away with it this time for Cathy as well. Finally we got rolling in Giallina and headed to Augustów at 9am.

We did not have a plan, except we were determined not to have a plan for the day, we would drive away and get lost somewhere. Which, considering the limited navigational aids at our disposal, was easily done. Having taken this decision we kept driving deeper into the Masurian forest.

We drove past several villages that had not been touched by the XX century. We passed more horses and wagons on the road than cars. Through the small towns, the asphalt turned to cobblestone, to my dismay as a driver, though the others enjoyed the picturesque sight. It added to the charm of the XIX century settings. Fields and fields of bright yellow dandelions!

We arrived at Augustów for lunch and ate at a totally nondescript place, very cheap: eggs, fatty sausages, cheese and tea and bread for 130 złoty for all four of us. We decided not to spend more time in this town with a majestic name but not much else to offer, at least to our naive western student eyes. Instead we thought we would try our luck in the luscious surrounding forests.

We then decided to have some kind of plan after all and take a cruise through the Augustów forest to Suwałki and Serny, but never made it to those cities. This was not meant to be a planned day, but an improvised one. The little dirt roads leading through the dense forests were too beguiling. At one point, I am not sure exactly where, it could have been any point on the route really, we veered off the main paved road into a dirt side path lined by tall trees. What heaven! The fresh cool smell of pines! Cathy and Ann went wild picking the delicate violets and tiny little white bell flowers.

Ann and I took turns standing on the seat and riding with our bodies sticking out through the open sunroof. We felt we could have spent all day that way. Eventually, we came to a clearing where various farms and pasture lands were. Unfortunately, there were bulls grazing in those pasture lands, so Ann was so kind to give way to me and let me out of the car and attract attention, how altruistic of her!

We wanted adventure and sure enough we got it, as for the second time in this trip we got hopelessly lost. Luckily this time we did not run into any Warsaw Pact military bases. There were no soldiers around, to our great relief, although this area was the stage for several immensely bloody battles between Germans and Russians at the beginning of World War I. There was no one around at all for many kilometers actually, I thought with somewhat less relief and mild apprehension. It was an eerie situation, with the huge trees projecting their long shadows and creating a tall dark green canopy that almost completely blocked our view of the sky. Stunning.

Eventually the road became too sandy to go further, so I turned the car around and headed back. However, we took the wrong fork somewhere (which proved once again my sense of directions was far from perfect) and ended up on another pitted dirt road. As we slowly tried to make our way out of there, two men came racing up to us on a tractor and almost assailed us. That they had a tractor was a fairly remarkable feat in itself, as almost all farmers we had seen in the region had their plows pulled by slow stocky horses. We weren't going anywhere too fast, so they came up to our window. One of them was a very old man, in his late eighties for sure, or at least he looked as if he was in his late eighties, or he could have been in his nineties for that matter.

Just a little flashback: a little earlier Ann had mentioned to us that she had relatives around Augustów, but did know where or what kind. So she told Cathy and me they were Dąbrowskis and Twardowskis. When these two characters approached, introducing themselves in a very drunken state, Ann tried to explain what connection she had to the area. They asked the name of her family and when she told them Dąbrowskis, the drunker of the two turned out to be a Dąbrowski, or at least he said he was. So I gleamed to Ann: "We found your uncle!". "God forbid," she responded.

We got talked into going to their house for tea. Uncle Dąbrowski led us to his farm, only a few hundred meters away, where he introduced us to his clan: three, possibly four generations of Masurian farmers. There was a really, really old lady dressed in black with a green shawl on her head, who did not speak much. Perhaps because she seemed not to hear much either. But she was very friendly and smiled a lot. Then there were a couple of very young kids, maybe five and three-years-old or something like that. They should be in school, I thought.

Tea turned out to be a spread of cakes, ham, bacon, bread and eggs. We heard the usual stories of some far distant cousin in America, of spending five years in a German camp, of how they hated the communists and the Russians and then we drank vodka. The very very old lady said she had spent seven or so years working in France and was extremely thrilled to use her French. She kept shaking her head over the drunken Dabrowski saying, in French, he was *"saoul comme un cochon"* (drunk like a pig).

Then another thin man wearing a threadbare beat-up jacket, I guessed the son of the very very old lady, in his forties maybe, became very friendly. He said we could stay with them for the night if we wanted, we were all welcome. The house was clearly not adequate to host four additional people, but I considered perhaps it could be a good experience and for a moment I thought of discussing this opportunity for a real immersion in a Polish rural family with my friends. In the end we politely replied that we did not want to disturb and insisted we needed to get back to Warsaw.

He insisted too, specifically indicating with his hands and eloquent smiles that Ann could spend the night with him in his room. Right. He must have been the father of the two kids, but where was his wife? Or maybe he was not, who knows, maybe he was a single uncle, but did it matter? He persisted, saying that Ann would not disturb him at all in his room, even if there was only one bed which the two of them could share no problem. At this point our eight eyes began to roll.

He really tried to persuade us that this would be best for all, as it was getting late in the day and it might be difficult for us to drive our way out of the forest and find a place to stay. His polite candor and his soft-spoken matter-of-factness in asking a foreign lady half his age to sleep with him before knowing as much as what her name was, I had to admit, quite disarming. One did not know exactly how to respond. Except that there was, of course, only one way to respond. At one point "uncle Dabrowski" kept staring at me and then insisted I looked Chinese.[25]

It was with some difficulty that we eventually managed to extricate ourselves from this excessively friendly company. Just as we

---

25 *This was the second time during my stay in Poland someone predicted my future connection with the Middle Kingdom. Maybe Poles, or at least some of them, have a way to see the future!*

were revving up to leave they gave us a sack of fresh eggs: Polish hospitality. After some trying, we even managed to get out of the forest and find a hotel to spend the night.

28 May 1980 – Wilanow and rubles

We returned to Warsaw and went to the Wilanow gardens with Marzena. Ann showed Cathy the Palace, which the rest of us had seen already, after which she managed to crash onto the steps of the magnificent architecture on her chin due to those slippery slippers they make one wear to protect their floors. Undeterred, we continued to play together in the gardens until early evening.

In the evening we went to see Marian and Ewa. We were warned by Marian (and others) not to even think of exchanging Soviet rubles in the black market, an activity we had grown accustomed to after months of Poland. All agreed it would be very risky. We had actually already bought some rubles from a classmate, but Marian pleaded to give them to him. And this was the master of smuggling! He would change them back into Polish money for us, or use them to buy caviar or whatever, but he became very serious and told us to never ever try and smuggle them across the Soviet border. For the only time ever, Marian did not say "OK!" and did not offer a way forward. So we decided to heed his advice and gave him the rubles.

29 May 1980 – Russian state exam

More errands, passport stamping to extend our Polish student visa at the police station and then dinner at Marzena's in the evening.

Most of our roommates were slightly worried today as they had exams coming up now and were diligently studying. This Saturday there was going to be some kind of Russian language State Examination which everyone had to pass with a 4 or 5 (out of 5) to graduate.

30 May 1980 – Train or plane?

Today Ann and Cathy wanted to buy their airplane tickets to go to Krakow. Cathy had not been there and Ann wanted to show that beautiful city to her. But to buy an airplane ticket in Poland, even a domestic flight ticket, you needed a passport. Or at least foreigners needed a passport. However Ann and Cathy did not have theirs as they were with the police in order to extend, yet one more time, our student visas. So no airplane tickets for them.

We then drove to the railway station, where the girls could buy a train ticket to Krakow, for which Andrew had discovered that, for some reason, they did not need a passport. Oh well, it would take longer but they would enjoy watching the rolling hills of the southern Polish landscape go by. They bought two tickets for the 3:00pm train.

To celebrate their accomplishment we went all together to the *winiarna* (wine bar) on the *Rynek Starego Miasta* (the central market square) at the heart of the old city of Warsaw. The choice of wines was average at best but prices, for us, were very low even for imported Italian and French wines.

After a pleasant stroll, a creamy ice cream at the nearby *Victoria* hotel concluded the morning. A couple of drunkards were hanging out by the hotel gate and they offered to wash our car while we licked our ice creams, which we readily accepted. Giallina badly needed a good scrub after the recent adventure in the muddy paths of the Masurian region.

Ice cream led to tea at Marzena's. Her mother insisted that we have lunch there but we did not want to take advantage one more time of their hospitality, which we knew cost them very dear. This time, somehow, I think it was the only time ever, we were able to excuse ourselves. Back home in our dorms, easy afternoon of rest.

Andrew, Romek and I had dinner at the *Bazyliszek* restaurant. These dinners at expensive (for the locals) restaurants had become so routine that I had almost completely stopped feeling ashamed about it. I confess I felt a bit guilty in the beginning of our term, we eating delicacies with so much penury around us, but that feeling went away quickly, especially as we realized that many Poles had unofficial ways to get what we were buying openly.

2 June 1980 – Bureaucracy and a wedding gift

This was one full day dedicated to jumping over bureaucratic hurdles. We picked up our passports at the police station, filled out forms for new visas for Cathy etc. Looked like we got everything, Polish extension to the end of our stay, Czechoslovak transit, Hungarian transit. No need for visa to go through Yugoslavia, a communist country but detached from the Soviet bloc and much more open to receive western visitors with no visa requirements.

Dinner at Marzena's, of course. We had actually considered inviting her to join us for the trip, to thank her and her family for her hospitality. Also, she spoke fluent Russian, which could come in handy. But there was no space in the backseat of Giallina, really. Moreover, she did not display any interest in the Soviet Union: she wanted to go west, not east.

Today we got our grades back. Mostly quite high, though a couple or professors seemed to have copped out and just handed politically correct grades for some reason: we all got the exact same grade in Foreign Policy and CMEA. It could be a coincidence, but I don't believe in coincidences.

We later went to see Marian, who said he would ship to Italy my "old" atlas and the crystal vase I bought. With a little tip to the customs officer my "antiques" bundle should make it through without problems.

Late at night, back in the dorm, we got a visit by Marta, the lady who had unsuccessfully tried to get into my bed (or Andrew's) for the last couple of months. She said she got engaged and was getting married soon. She did not say with whom, but somehow I would have bet my last złoty he was not Polish. Anyway I was happy for her, she was a fine lady, and I was happy for us as well, because this meant she would stop chasing the two of us.

As a wedding gift we gave her the floor lamp we had bought last February. We would be leaving soon and would not be needing it any more. The days were getting longer in northern Europe, little use for a lamp anyway, quite a contrast with the long dark nights of winter. She readily accepted and appreciated, the newlyweds had to furnish a house now! Good luck Marta, and congratulations!

3. THE BEETLE DRIVES TO THE USSR

3 June 1980 – Off to the USSR

Early rise today, it was going to be a long one. Just to make sure we were adequately alert for the occasion and start on an upbeat note, we took a cold shower, as there was no hot water in the dorm. After which Andrew and I loaded up Giallina and picked up the ladies at the *Sabinki* dorm. Ann lamented she had not had any hot water for a month and had to use a kettle to wash her hair. Then the four of us drove to Marzena's for a full Polish breakfast. We would miss her and her family for the next few weeks. After that we filled up with some black market gas and off we went, eastward bound.

We reached the Polish border station at Terespol very easily. After some perfunctory checks of our papers the Polish soldiers, looking slightly bemused, let us go with an easy *niema problemu*, (no problem). By 1:00pm we slowly drove on a bridge across the Bug river and were met by the Soviet border guards on the other side.

Here things took quite a long time. We saw some French tourists who had just finished to have themselves and their car thoroughly inspected. They were coming out of a small building next to the parking area where we stopped. Ann and I tried to ask a few questions, but the Soviet guards told us we were not allowed to talk to them. After a few minutes we saw them again in a quiet corner of the border station, away from the guards, as they were getting ready to drive on and did talk to them more extensively anyway. We asked questions like "did they search you everywhere?" and got a nod in response, apparently they had been strip searched and they also said even their car's spare tire had been taken apart and inspected inside!

As we waited for our turn to be searched, Andrew and I played American football in the parking area. Some Soviet soldiers who were not directly involved in the searches watched us slightly bewildered but said nothing. I guessed they were more curious about a game that was not played in their country than interested in showing authority. And I imagined there was no specific regulation that forbade playing American football at border crossing stations.

When our turn came, Giallina was thoroughly inspected, they even took apart her air filter (Giallina was an original VW Beetle model, powered by an air-cooled engine placed in the rear of the car). They opened everything, looked everywhere, under the seats, inside the seats, and of course through all of our luggage. With the same care, it must be said, they meticulously put everything back in its place at the end. Thankfully they did not strip search any of us!

In the meantime, I chatted a bit with an officer who seemed friendlier than the others. He even let me try his military hat on! It was too small for me. That was always going to be a problem for me, my head was size 60, XXL, and quite often I could not buy a hat I liked because they did not have a big enough size. I would like to buy one as a souvenir for this trip, they were quite beautiful. I thought I would try to exchange some of the special hard currency (stockings, jeans) we had with us. But maybe not right here at the border station. Maybe with some other soldier, or flea market dealer, during our stay in the USSR.

We spoke in Polish; my Polish had improved from nil to a simple conversational level after three months of practice, and I wondered how he learned his. Maybe he lived near the border and was in frequent contact with Polish traders. Or maybe he came from a family that used to be Polish: before World War II the border was more than one hundred kilometers to the east of here. Both banks of the Bug river were in Poland.

After all the checks were completed, we met with a guy from *Intourist* (the Soviet government agency which had a monopoly on all foreign incoming tourists) who gave us all kinds of detailed instructions about our trip. He repeated to us what we had been told in Warsaw: all hotels and camping sites had been pre-booked for us, and we were not allowed to seek accommodation elsewhere. We were to stay on the direct route between all the cities we would visit. However, we were allowed to drive around as we pleased within each city. Very clear.

Finally, at 5:00 o'clock, after a good four hours at the border station, we were free to go and hit the road in Bielorussia, or the White Russian Soviet Republic, and headed straight for the capital, Minsk. We were quite excited to have entered the territory of this mysterious country about which we had read so much but we had never visited before. Come to think of it, I am pretty sure none of us had ever even met anyone who had visited the USSR before. Smooth driving initially, but not for long.

After a few kilometers a couple of policemen stopped us for speeding. I was driving at 90 km/h, which seemed reasonable on this highway, but apparently the speed limit (not shown on any sign that we could see along the way) was 60 km/h. Or so they said. They glanced at our papers, had a careful look at Giallina from all sides and let us go. I got the impression that they were just curious about this kind of bright yellow foreign car, of which they must not see many. In fact we did not see any other foreign car all day.

It was only a few months after the Soviet invasion of Afghanistan had frozen contacts between East and West in Europe and while I did not have statistics to compare with previous years, I imagined tourism must have suffered accordingly. In any case, tourism mostly consisted of package tours, very few individual visas were issued and even fewer for independent travel by private car.

After about 100 km the four-lane highway merged into one lane in each direction and a bit later it was completely interrupted because of some road work. Interesting to note that it was mostly (perhaps only) women who seemed to do the hard work with spades and wheelbarrows carrying and spreading tar. A few men were chatting by the road side.

Because of the road works, we had to leave the highway that had been assigned to us for a side road, thus directly contravening the unambiguous instructions we had just received a few minutes earlier, but we had no choice. And to make matters worse, we did not know where to go: there were no road signs, in any language, about a detour or on how to go back to the highway after the road works interruption. We were stuck and had no idea what we should do. The clock was ticking, it would soon be dark and the memory of our arrest in the Warsaw Pact military base in Czechoslovakia was still quite vivid in our minds.

To complete our rather gloomy "welcome to the USSR" picture, it started raining quite hard. At one point a lightening hit so close to us the car jumped. Really.

For a fleeting second I thought of driving back to the Polish border. I really did not want to be interrogated by the KGB. Moreover, while the three of us "veterans" would probably be able to handle an interrogation, Cathy was not likely to hold up as well.

Eventually, in the best possible outcome, we would be sent back to the border anyway. However, as I drove in the rain, I discarded the idea and did not even mention it to the others. We had spent too much time and money planning for this trip to give up so soon, and our expectations were very high. In fact I was a bit ashamed for having contemplated that option, and I debated whether I should include it in this book, but here it is. Undeterred by guards, muddy road work sites or heavy rain and lightening, we drove on.

Luckily, after a short while we managed to stop a truck and the driver pointed us to a secondary road that led us to Minsk. Take the "old road" he said to Ann, the only one among us who could try to understand him. We needed fuel, but several half-built gas stations along the way displayed signs that read "under construction". We were forced to leave even the secondary road and take a really narrow dirt path that ended in a small village where, to our relief, a gas station was open for business, and we finally could fill up our tank. From there, somehow, our map-less selves found our way back to the highway. Andrew's sense of directions and orientation, always better than mine, helped. We should have had a compass but who would think of carrying a compass to drive in Europe in this day and age?

We finally reached our camping ground by the evening and got settled into our two bungalows. They were OK though the bathrooms were pretty disgusting and there was no toilet paper. Oh well, I had been a boy scout after all, I would survive! Few tourists to be seen, it was a quiet place. Our accommodation was simple but adequate for the night. No hot water though, well one can't always have everything. The weather became more gentle, it stopped raining. Fairly basic dinner, after which we went to bed quite early, it had been a long and tiring day.

4 June 1980 – Minsk to Smolensk: Afghanistan, Bulgarian wine and the Moscow Olympics

After a leisurely breakfast we got moving at 11:00. From our bucolic location in the suburbs we drove into the city and then around downtown Minsk, and found it majestic in its own way, built to be grand, but often dull. The high points of the tour were a couple of huge monuments, inevitable refrains in all Soviet conurbations: one to Lenin and another to victory in World War II. Good weather tough, warm and sunny, we could open Giallina's sunroof and enjoy the breeze.

For lunch we had some dark bread and butter. Russian bread enjoys a good reputation and the loaf we consumed stood up to it. We washed it down with strong coffee into which we poured a generous amount of sugar and milk. As an Italian I consider it a sacrilege to have anything resembling a cappuccino after 11 o'clock in the morning but here I made an exception and I must say it was rather agreeable. No hot water though, well one can't always have everything.

When at some point we wanted to drink water we were directed to some public dispensers that were ubiquitous, as we would find out, throughout the USSR. They looked like big refrigerators, which I think they were, and were placed on the pavement or in public areas like gardens or parks. I was puzzled by the fact that each refrigerator was equipped with a set of glasses meant for public use and shared by the whole population. A thirsty person would approach the water fridge, insert a kopek (1 cent of a ruble) take a glass, put it upside down on a metal grid and push down: the glass would be rinsed by a sprinkle of water shooting upward. Then one would turn the glass up, place it under the tap, dispense the water and drink it, after which the quenched citizen would leave the glass upside down the for the next person to use. The machines I saw dispensed fizzy water.

As we drove around, one policeman stopped us because I was trying to make a right turn from the middle lane of a wide boulevard. I had signaled my intention to turn (I think I did anyway) and I was very careful and waited for the road to be clear before turning, but still, it was, technically, a traffic violation. In Rome no one would even notice.

He was initially a bit brusque but when he found out who we were and where we come from we started speaking Polish and it all ended with big smiles, a pat in the back, and, more importantly, no fine to pay. Again, similarly to yesterday, as we drove away I thought that rather than punishing my traffic violation he was just curious to meet funny-looking foreigners in a yellow Volkswagen beetle. So we had been stopped twice in two days by Soviet traffic police, not bad.

We hit the road again in the direction of Smolensk after a quick lunch, just when it started raining heavily. The French couple who had been going through Soviet customs yesterday just before us were driving right behind, obviously we had the same itinerary toward Moscow. I would have like to ask them what they did when they found the road construction on the way to Minsk.

At our assigned Smolensk accommodation we were very warmly greeted by a group of students who ran the camping site. Although from here to Leningrad we were supposed to have tents, they gave us bungalows tonight for some reason. Free upgrade. Thank God because it was freezing!

Three of the students spoke good English and seemed to be especially eager to socialize with us: Lena, Natasha and Sergey. They were on a summer working holiday or something like that. A program set up by or connected to the *Komsomol*, the Soviet Communist Party's youth organization. Our banter and casual talk accompanied by simple but pleasant Bulgarian wine dragged on for several hours. Their English was surprisingly good.

Only a couple of times the discussion became a bit tense, when we touched the question of the Soviet invasion of Afghanistan. Sergey insisted Soviet forces were providing brotherly help to the Afghan socialist government whose proletarian revolution was threatened by foreign imperialist agents led by the United States: pure party line.

In reality the communist and pro-Soviet government led by Amin, which had overthrown the communist but not-sufficiently-pro-Soviet government led by Taraki, had in its own turn been replaced by another communist, Karmal, whom the Soviets thought they could trust better than the other two. He was installed at gunpoint in December 1979 when Moscow sent in the Red Army to occupy the whole country and had Amin killed only weeks after he had killed Taraki. If it sounds a bit complicated and abstruse, it's because it is.

I would not have been surprised to learn that the CIA was involved in one way or another, but this was really a struggle amongst different communist factions in Afghanistan. The Soviet Union probably figured that, if the unpredictable civil struggle continued, others might have taken advantage. Maybe the Americans, maybe the Chinese or, why not?, the Pakistanis. With regional power Iran distracted by its own upheaval following he Islamic revolution of last year, the temptation to go in and sort it out must have been irresistible.

The other, related, topic of lively discussion was the upcoming Moscow Olympics. Our hosts insisted sport and politics should be kept separate. Western countries, as I mentioned earlier, were poised to boycott the games because of Soviet invasion of Afghanistan, and this politicization ran counter to the spirit of the Olympics. Again Sergey was the most passionate of the three in this conversation, while Lena and Natasha did not seem to be so interested in political discussions. They were probably right.

I thought here Sergey had a point. I agreed there was no reason to spoil the games, especially as it had already been decided that the next games, in 1984, would be held in the United States, in Los Angeles, and the Soviets would probably return the favor and spoil those games too, even if that meant missing out on their usual haul of prestigious medals.[26]

Our hosts also believed that China (Moscow's communist rival) got a bloody nose in Vietnam (Moscow's communist friend) last year when it launched its "punitive" campaign following the Vietnamese invasion of Cambodia. Since 1975 Cambodia had been governed by the pro-Chinese Communist regime of the *Khmer Rouge*, perhaps the most bloodthirsty dictatorship of modern times. Vietnam was communist, of course, and had its hands free from the war it has just won against the United States, but it was a pro-Soviet communist and, for centuries, it had been wary of its large Chinese neighbor. In 1979 Vietnam intervened in Cambodia, drove the pro-China *Khmer Rouge* up the mountains and installed another, pro-Soviet, communist government in Phnom Penh.

Here the historical truth was somewhat more blurred, and lots of Chinese and Vietnamese soldiers died for no reason until the Chinese pulled back from Vietnam. Both sides, of course, celebrated victory, though nothing changed: the border between Vietnam and China stayed were it was before the conflict except for a tiny area taken by China. So did the Vietnamese-installed regime in Phnom Penh, much to the chagrin of the United States, which after the death of Mao Zedong began to see a possible ally in communist China and its friends against pro-Soviet communist Vietnam. Funny twists of the Cold War.

---

26 *That is exactly what would happen, with the result that two Olympic games were spoiled by the absence of major national teams.*

Be all of that as it may, the point I took away from this conversation was that the young people we had met actually still believed in communism and in the leading role of the USSR, in one way or another. Not a single one of the many Poles I met over the last few months had anything positive to say about communism or the USSR, though one or two or Ann's acquaintances, she told me, did.

5 June 1980 – Smolensk to Moscow: Red Square at night

In the morning we visited the Smolensk cathedral, one of the oldest in Russia. As we would find out over the next couple of weeks, it was also one of the relatively few to be both in good condition and open to the faithful as well as to visitors.

As we approached on foot from a nearby lot, where we had parked Giallina, an old lady, head covered in a black scarf, was crawling on her fours on the wet ground, inching her way toward the church. It must have been some kind of penance she was going through to punish her body for her sins. It reminded me of those catholics who, at least in the old times, climbed on their knees on the *Scala Sancta* (holy staircase) in Rome to repent for their sins. It was hard for me to imagine what this fragile god-fearing woman could possibly have done to deserve this kind of painful punishment but here she was. A young blond kid, perhaps ten years-old, briskly walked past her on his way. The contrast between the old and the new generations could not have been starker.

Once inside the church, another old woman had no sins to repent for and instead screamed at me for taking some pictures. And yet, unlike so many other places we would visit in the USSR, here it was not forbidden to photograph the building and its art. So I clicked away a couple of times and then gave up as I did not want to get into an argument and anyway she was definitely more at home here than me, maybe photos offended her spirituality.

We then drove on to Moscow. This time the car with our French travel mates was just ahead of us. Funny we kept meeting them on the road but not while touring our destinations. We reached our camping ground by the middle of the afternoon. It was raining hard and it was very cold. Gee, it was early June!

The staff greeted us with tea and offered bungalows to us instead of tents if we paid a small extra money, which we did as the wintery temperature made any thought of sleeping in a tent utterly unappealing. We ate at their restaurant and hit the road one more time to go to town.

This was easier than expected as the very long road where our accommodation was situated, Kalinin Prospekt, led straight to the Red Square and the Kremlin: the historical, political and religious heart of Moscow! We got there in no time and easily found a parking spot by the square, traffic was very light.

At a first glance, the Square and the adjacent Kremlin were by far the main attraction of the city, which was otherwise pretty gloomy, oppressively grey and characterless. The Red Square however, so called after the color of the October Revolution, had an impressive and majestic feel to it. On one side the Kremlin, the old citadel (*Kreml* in Russian means "citadel") that was the fulcrum of Soviet power ever since the capital was moved from Leningrad (then Saint Petersburg) to Moscow in 1918, soon after the October Revolution.[27]

On the other side of the square the majestic profile of the Saint Basil cathedral, now a museum. The USSR officially being an atheist state, few churches were allowed to operate normally. The Russian Orthodox church had never completely been erased from the map, or from the hearts of many Russians for that matter, but since 1918 it had been relegated to the margins of society. Only for a brief time during a time in World War II, when things looked desperate enough, did Stalin reach out to request the Orthodox Pope's support in the national effort to fight the Axis invaders. Once the war was over, Stalin did not acknowledge his contribution and went back to persecuting the faithful as before.[28]

On one side of the Kremlin's wall, about half way the length of the square, stood the mausoleum to Lenin, the founding father of the Soviet Union. One of the founding fathers, really, but the only one who was not subsequently either purged, assassinated or otherwise

---

27 *Moscow had been the capital for centuries until Peter the Great founded St Petersburg and moved the capital there in 1712.*
28 *Saint Basil became a UNESCO World heritage Site in 1990 and would again be used for occasional religious services after the dissolution of the USSR in 1991.*

erased from history and forever denigrated as an aberration to the ideals of socialism. He was the iconic symbol that no one had dared to tarnish, and thousands of people lined up on the Red Square to see his embalmed body inside. Stalin's grave, on the other hand, only got a little hole in the wall of the citadel, you would hardly notice unless you were really looking for it.

After a brief exploratory walk around Red Square we visited the GUM (*Gosudarstvennyi Universál'nyj Magazín*, or State FN Universal Store), the most famous (or infamous?) shopping mall in the USSR.[29] Lots of shops in a decrepit old structure that had seen grander days, but hardly anything was available to buy. The huge building had been conceived as a covered market in the XIX century, similarly to other comparable structures in Europe. It was then converted to office space by Stalin in the 1920s, to host the staff in charge of the Five-Year Plans that were supposed to organize socialist production after the wholesale nationalizations of the previous years. Only in the 1953, a few months after Stalin's death, was GUM again reopened as a retail shopping mall.

Today the scene which it presented to us was depressing. Each shop was properly staffed by two or three salespeople, but they were hardly doing any sales at all. It seemed to us their main occupation was chatting with each other to kill time. There was not much more they could do even if they wanted to, as the shelves were mostly barren of any goods. It was much worse than comparable malls in Warsaw, and that was saying something.

At some point we heard the sound of boots marching on the cobblestone and saw a small company of Soviet soldiers dressed up in parade uniform who were marching slowly, solemnly, toward Lenin's tomb. Quite a few people gathered around to see the hourly change of the guard. It was in fact quite a show. The soldiers were trained to perform perfect twists and turns and in less than a blink of an eye the newly arrived guards had replaced the ones who had stood there for the previous hour, serious and perfectly immobile.

As we strolled around the square, one guy named Igor, about our age, introduced himself to us and asked Andrew to sell him the

---

[29] *After the collapse of the USSR, and the massive privatizations of the 1990s, the word "State" was replaced with "Central", Glavnyi in Russian, thus reflecting the new economic realities while at the same time keeping the same universally accepted acronym.*

jeans he was wearing. Andrew might well have considered the deal, we could use some rubles and his jeans would be easily replaced once back home. But he could not carry it through without risking arrest for indecent exposure. Undeterred, he did exchange an American wild-west-style belt buckle with a picture of a buffalo for one that Igor had taken from a Soviet army belt that sported a star with the unmistakable hammer and sickle logo.

As luck had it I happened to have some extra pairs of jeans in the car. I had brought them with me to wear them, they were my size, but also to take advantage of situations like this which I expected would present themselves. I sold three pairs to him for 350 rubles, quite a considerable sum of money.

The cash would be useful for the odd purchase in the coming two weeks, even though money could not buy much in this country. Prices were generally low, but shelves were empty. Unless you had connections, preferably in the Communist Party, you could not buy much at all with money, with a few exceptions as we would discover later.

Purchasing power in the USSR was measured with the yardstick of your ability to *access* to whatever it was you wanted to buy, not with the amount of money necessary to *pay* for it. Access could be the black market, or just special shops the access to which was limited to the members of the *nomenklatura*, the hierarchy of card-carrying members of the Communist Party. The higher you ranked in the system, the more access you had to goods and services which were not otherwise openly available, no matter how much money you had.

Igor was very friendly and we spent a few hours walking around the Red Square together. He was ready to talk about just about anything in his good English, except politics. Associating with western capitalists was generally not a badge of honor, and discussing politics could be dangerous. Dangerous for us, if he was an intelligence operative under cover who had been sent out to figure us out, which was in fact reasonably likely. Or dangerous for him, if he was not a spy and someone should overhear unorthodox conversations, or if one of us was a CIA spook, which, for all he knew, was also a possibility.

As we walked around, several people stopped us along the way and asked for chewing gum, but we did not have any. Silly us, should have known better. We knew that such luxury items, typical of decadent capitalist bourgeois economies, commanded a premium price in the controlled socialist economy and we should have brought some along to exchange for local stuff like premium caviar from the Caspian Sea or Red Army military clothes and accessories that were in ample supply.

Lots of policemen could be seen all over the place. At one point two of them stopped us and, it seemed, almost everyone else within their reach, for no apparent reason. They asked a few general questions about what we were doing, where we came from etc. and then let us go. A bit like what was happening in Italy in these years of terrorism, except that in Italy the police was looking for suspected fascist or communist extremists. Here there were no terrorists to speak of.

We were back at our camping ground fairly late, and went to sleep right away! It seemed these first couple of days in the USSR were very intense, lots to do and see, and quite a bit of driving to get from one city to another. But we were determined to make the best of our limited time available, we did not know when, or whether, we would have another opportunity for an experience like this.

6 June 1980 – Moscow: books, champagne and army belts

Got up late and drove straight into the city again. We decided to have brunch at a restaurant of the *Arbat* hotel, not bad, and got quite a good deal for chicken at only 4 rubles, about 1 dollar. There wasn't much choice but, perhaps because this was a hotel frequented by many foreigners, there was enough quantity and quality for an adequate meal.

Next up was a visit to the *Dom Knigi* (House of the Book), the biggest book store in Moscow. An official, state-run business, with lots of propaganda and political books, mostly in Russian but some in English and other languages. I was not so interested in these, but I did buy some posters.

The Soviets always loved political posters, they were famous for this kind of communication medium, and produced excellent ones over many decades. Maybe it had to do with the need for propaganda, or maybe artists who worked for a dictatorship, and believed in the cause, were especially inspired. Many posters from Fascist Italy were equally evocative and artistically exquisite. However, those from Nazi Germany were always more sinister and spine-chilling somehow. Those from Maoist China were more similar to their Soviet counterparts, but generally not as emotionally powerful, at least not the ones I had seen, which was not many.

Many posters in the shop carried relatively uncontroversial historical overtones, like for example those on the victory in World War II. Or those of smiling papa Lenin playing with children. Everyone likes children right? Lenin was the last, and almost the only, Soviet leader to be represented in posters. All subsequent leaders had been discredited by their respective successors, so there was no Stalin on any poster, no Khrushchev and no current leader either. Of course no foreign leader: no Mao, no Fidel Castro, not even the charismatic Che Guevara. For all one could criticize the USSR for, at least one could say there was no personality cult in the country today. Anyway, it would have been really hard for any artist to create any sort of emotionally charged poster with someone as dull and dour as President and party General Secretary Leonid Brezhnev.

Some posters were more general in their subject matter, like for example those that dealt with socialism as a force of peace in the world. I bought a victory in World War II series of posters, a set of prints with Lenin and the children and a green poster with a bottle of liquor and a quotation by Seneca which warned that excessive consumption of alcohol amounted to suicide. How true, especially here.

We met Igor again late in the afternoon and together with him we all went to the *Kosmos* hotel for a drink of *sovietskoe shampanskoe* (8 rubles). It was made in Crimea, a peninsula off southern Ukraine, and it tasted a bit on the sweet side. And they had no qualms in calling it "champagne" as the USSR, of course, did not have to abide by any European Economic Community rules on protected denominations.

Over a glass of bubbly we talked about the upcoming Olympics, and Igor said he read on the *Pravda* (the official newspaper of the Communist Party, it meant "Truth", even though it usually printed everything but) that all western countries were going to participate with their full complement of athletes after all, and that they would bring along their flags and play their national anthems, and that therefore the US boycott had been a failure. Sounded strange to me, the *International Herald Tribune* (the international joint venture by the *New York Times* and the *Washington Post*) reported Italy and the UK were sending athletes but without flags. France, adopting a more distinct policy as always, was indeed going with its flag. West Germany had not made up its ind yet. We would have to wait and see. Perhaps there was still time for a solution so that all could go and compete and we could all enjoy a proper Olympics, but it did not seem likely.

I exchanged five packs of American Salem cigarettes for a Soviet army belt that Igor conveniently happened to have in his pocket. I never smoked cigarettes, but they were just as good as currency here. Actually better: if you had cigarettes, you could smoke them, while if you had money you would have to buy them first, which was not something to be taken for granted.

Driving around the city, to get a feel of the atmosphere, was not especially rewarding: dull and boring. Several policemen made it more lively by repeatedly stopping us to check our documents as we drove around. There were some avenues with twelve lanes (yes twelve!) and it was impossible to change lane fast enough to take a turn, especially at some huge roundabouts. So sometimes I changed lanes a bit too fast and they inevitably stopped our car, asked for all our papers, gave me a dirty look and let us go.

The building of the Council of Mutual Economic Assistance (CMEA, or Comecon), shaped like an open book, provided a rare example of modern architecture with an original twist.[30]

In the evening we looked for a restaurant to have dinner, but by 21:30 most were closed. We ended up in a small and very forgettable greasy spoon before heading back to the camping ground in the suburbs.

7 June 1980 – Hard currency shopping, Kremlin museum and Bolshoi dancers

Lazy morning and lunch at the famous *Rossiya* (Russia) hotel, disappointing. Much (most?) of what was on the menu was not available. After repeated answers of "we don't have" by the waiter at each of our successive attempts to order a dish, we asked him to let us know what they did have. Some mediocre cuts of chewy meat and

---

30 *After the demise of the Comecon the building became the headquarters of the government of the city of Moscow.*

potatoes was the best we could get a hold of. And this was in a highly visible place smack in the center of the capital, which you would think they would understand was a kind of shop window of the country. I had naively imagined they would have made a special effort to stock up the refrigerators of the iconic Rossiya. But they did not. Maybe they could not. Or maybe they did but the best food was reserved for the authorities and special dignitaries, VIP guests of the Communist Party and the like, none of which categories we obviously belonged to.

We then visited the *Beriozka* (little birch) shop, that sold all kinds of stuff that was much in demand in the USSR but taken for granted by us. Things like record players, good toothpaste, American cigarettes. They were special shops where you could buy what you could not find in other, normal, shops. These shops had a long history and existed in several Communist countries (we had been using *Pewex* in Poland) but here they had a special transgressive flair, maybe because most Soviet citizens were not allowed in.

Prices were quite high, really the same as in the West and much more expensive than Poland for certain items: for example a beautiful book on the Kremlin that I had luckily bought in Warsaw for 430 złoty (15 dollars) here cost 40 dollars. In fact they sold quite a few beautiful art and photography books, Soviet authored and Soviet produced, that were not available to normal Soviet consumers in regular bookstores. I did buy a few and was very happy with them, good quality paper and color reproductions of the country's art treasures.

We then went inside the Kremlin for another walk. Lots of soldiers were marching around. There were many churches in the citadel, but they were ALL closed. Every single one of them. We could read *NA REMONT* (meaning "under restoration") on numerous metal plates hanging on the doors of the various churches. They were officially referred to as "cathedrals": from the curiously named *Dormition*, to the more predictable *Archangel* and *Annunciation*, they were all located around the unimaginatively named Cathedrals Square. In the end the square was the only place we could step on, the façades and domes of the churches the only things we could see, from the outside, as we could not visit any cathedral inside.

We tried to buy tickets for the famous "multifaceted palace" the most majestic and richly decorated of the many buildings in the citadel, but they told us tickets were sold out for the day and advised to book several weeks in advance. We knew this venue was used for official government ceremonies, so maybe there was some foreign leaders expected today, no way of knowing. No luck. However we were treated to a free show of thousands of people lining up in Red Square to visit Lenin's mausoleum. We quickly dismissed the thought of standing in line for hours to get a glimpse of the embalmed body of the first Soviet leader. I would have liked to go in, not so much to see Lenin but to see people's expressions and reactions in his presence. But we had so much else to see and do, so we gave up on Vladimir Ilych Ulyanov, as he was officially known.

We all felt a bit down because we had not been able to get inside any Kremlin building yet, and kept walking along the Kremlin wall, chatting with Igor. He told us that it was very difficult for a Soviet citizen to travel abroad. First, you had to apply to travel to a specific country to the local police station, and they would apply for a visa on your behalf to the relevant foreign consulate.

Then, after you had a visa, you could apply for a passport. Strange, hard to believe in fact, that any embassy would issue a visa to someone without seeing a passport first. Anyway it was well known that it was difficult for Soviet citizens in 1980 to travel abroad for tourism, and most of the few who did so were part of a handful of organized tours. Private trips abroad were quite rare and usually required an invitation by someone in the country to be visited, who would sponsor the Soviet tourist and take all responsibility for food, shelter, health care and transportation back to the USSR. Igor did not seem too upset by these limitations though, he considered them normal. To us, they seemed absurd. Maybe he was a spy after all.

After a while, while we were still walking around the Kremlin, without a real goal in mind as we could not get into either churches or palaces, we saw a small door that was half-way open. We were not sure what that building was. There were a couple of guards at the door but they looked quite relaxed and mostly intent at chatting with each other. We decided to try our luck and casually walked through the door, we thought something worth seeing had to be inside if they put two guards on duty.

The guards noticed us and came to meet us, speaking Russian and indicating fairly unequivocally that we had to leave. I replied to them in Italian (I guessed that perhaps as an Italian I had a better chance than if we were identified as Americans) and with my hands that we were tourists, we were in Moscow only for a few days, and we wanted to see more of the Kremlin.

I was about to say I was a devout communist and a friend of the Soviet Union but that would not have been very credible with three Americans by my side. Moreover, even Italian communists were no longer so pro-Soviet by 1980. After the Soviet and Warsaw Pact invasion of Czechoslovakia in 1968 the Italian Communist Party, together with the Spanish, Portuguese and French brothers, had launched *Eurocommunism,* a kind of hybrid doctrine trying to marry communism with capitalist democracy. It never made much sense to me, but that was another story.

As we were pondering our next move, some stranger, a Russian guy, who had seen our interaction with the guards came around and started talking to them. I was not sure what they talked about for the next few minutes, though clearly it was about us. At the end of it all the guards escorted us to a ticket office where we could buy what they said were the very last three discounted student tickets available on that day and a regular ticket. The cost of the tickets was negligible, a few kopeks, or cents of rubles. As so often in the country, power lied in access to goods and services, not in the money to buy them. We did not have the faintest idea of who the man who talked the guards into letting us in was, nor why he did it. By the time we had tickets in our hands he was gone forever. At that point we learned we were at the entrance of the Kremlin's museum of the Tsars' imperial armory.

Once inside our jaws dropped at unison. There was a fantastic display the Tsars' ceremonial weapons and armor, fur coats, robes, furniture, carriages, etc. Absolutely stunning. There was a separate museum for the jewels of the imperial family but that required yet another ticket and we could not get it today. We were unfortunately not allowed to take photos, but it was a sight we would never forget.

In the evening, we were lucky to get tickets to an amazing performance in the Congress Palace theater of the Kremlin: a dance program by the Bolshoi ballet, one of the most famous in the world. Much, much better than anything I had ever seen before, or that I was likely to see again any time soon. The Bolshoi more than lived up to its reputation. So much better than the one we saw in Warsaw. The theater was fairly full and the public was very well behaved. There was absolute silence during the performance. I wish I could say the same of concert halls in Italy.

8 June 1980 – Highway driving and Novgorod churches

It was sadly time to leave the capital and head north. We departed in the morning in the direction of Novgorod. We would miss Igor for the rest of our trip, he was fun and quite informative if always somewhat stiff in his statements whenever the subject became even remotely sensitive from a political point of view. But then again who knows, maybe he was a KGB operative, haha, no I did not really think so but it was not inconceivable. So few tourists these days, and four kids from NATO countries, including no fewer than three Americans, driving around freely in a yellow Volkswagen? Very suspicious! But even if he was a spook, he was good company anyway.

It was a long ride and the road was of mediocre quality at best. About 50 km out of Moscow we were slowed down and then had to stop altogether, there was some road work on the highway. Again, as we had seen before just after we entered the USSR near Minsk, most, in fact, ALL workers are women. The workers who worked that is, shoving smoking hot tar and operating machines. There was plenty of male road workers just lying down by the roadside and looking on. Really, I could not believe my eyes, they were laying belly down, elbows on the ground, chin on the palm of their hands, looking on as their female colleagues slaved away with their spades in the tar.

Anyway, after witnessing and photographing some of the work of the unsmiling (I would not smile either in their position) stocky Soviet ladies, we could see all vehicles ahead of us were re-routed to a secondary, much smaller road. When we approached the diversion and prepared to do the same, however, the man who was sending everyone for the detour flagged us to go straight through and stay on the main highway. Just us. Everyone else was diverted.

Such a privilege! Why? I imagined they did not want to show foreign capitalists poorly paved secondary roads that would make the country look bad. Not sure, but it was just easier to keep driving on instead of taking the detour. Of course we had no proper map and again the memory of our thrilling detour in Czechoslovakia came to our mind. Our black sense of humor was given easy material by our situation: we joked about spending the night drinking vodka with the stocky ladies road workers, or contradicting each other in Russian and ending up in Siberia for trespassing socialist military areas. We imagined what local military commanders would think if somehow they were informed that we had already trespassed a military base less than four months earlier.

But we did not need to worry and just kept driving, splendidly alone, on this newly surfaced shiny black highway. The only problem was that the tar was so fresh much of it got thrown up by Giallina's tires and ended up sticking to her pristine yellow sides. It would take a lot of work to clean it up when we got around to it.

At some point we were not alone any more, as we were overtaken by a very official-looking convoy of black cars, led by two big Mercedes Benz sedans (the first we had seen in the USSR) with police markings.

Usually the police had *Ladas*, the clanky FIATs made in Togliatti. This is a city named after Palmiro Togliatti, the boss of the Italian Communist Party from the 1930s to his death – in Soviet Crimea – in 1964. The Agnelli family, the hyper-capitalist bosses of Italy's largest car maker, agreed to establish a factory there 1966. The result was the *Lada*, a cheap car that was produced for the next two decades in the millions and for most Soviets was the only chance to own wheels.

Anyway cars produced in Togliatti were not good enough for these VIPs. This must have been an important convoy but they were too fast for us to try and peek inside and maybe try to recognize a Politburo member or two.

When we reached Novgorod we settled down in our assigned camping ground then headed to town. Lots of small churches, I counted at least twenty, all next to each other in the central part of the town. Why would Novgorod, or any city really, need to pack so much church in such a small area was beyond us. And, like the cathedrals in the Moscow Kremlin, they were ALL shut down *NA REMONT*, for restoration. It was one of the first Russian words I learned and I read it so many times they made sure I would never forget it. Could not get a foot into any one of them at all.

We could have visited one actually: it had been converted to a museum on the "Truth about religion" no less, but by now I had had enough of communist propaganda and did not go, my loss! I am not sure whether any of the others went in, but I don't think so as no one talked about it ever after.

Ended the evening with a *scopa* tournament which kept us awake for a long time. Later, when we went to bed, the mosquitoes did for quite a bit longer.

9 June 1980 – Novgorod to Leningrad, black market, caviar and Soviet champagne

We spent the morning driving and walking around Novgorod. Picked up some cokes on the roadside. A little old lady was thrilled to sit down and talk with us, she wanted to practice pronouncing English words. She said she was preparing herself for the Olympic tourists expected in great numbers later in the year.

The first peculiarity that jumped to my attention was the number of monuments erected all around the city to glorify military equipment, mostly of the heavy kind: tanks, artillery, anti-aircraft guns from World War II, which here was referred to as the "Great Patriotic War".

And of course to the universally loved (except by Axis soldiers perhaps) *Katyusha* multiple rocket launchers, a symbol of Soviet resistance to nazi-fascist aggression and ultimate victory. It was affectionately referred to as "Stalin's organ" because its parallel metallic rocket launching tubes resembled the musical instrument. What probably not many Soviets knew was that Georgy Langemak, the engineer who designed the *Katyusha*, died without seeing the achievements of his invention: he was accused of treason and summarily executed during Stalin's purges in 1938, before the war even started, only to be posthumously rehabilitated in the 1950s.

A war monument on the city's Kremlin was guarded by young children, about ten to twelve-year-old kids, who performed a change of the guard with an elaborate goose-stepping choreography like the adult guards at the Kremlin in Moscow who guarded Lenin's mausoleum. Some other *Young Pioneers* were marching up and down the central avenues of the city.

We had lunch in a restaurant in the Kremlin, a charming building that was a converted old orthodox church! All other churches were still closed *na remont*, for restoration. But no one was working at restoring them, it seemed there was no hurry to put them back into religious service, or visits by tourists for that matter, anytime soon. We treated ourselves to champagne and a succulent deboned chicken in cream sauce described to us as "transfiguration style". The name probably referred to the transfiguration of Jesus, who appeared radiant to the apostles after praying together with them on top of a mountain. Perhaps it was just the old name of the church now used as a restaurant.

After lunch we hit the road again, direction Leningrad. The route was poorly signposted and once we got close to Leningrad we were lost, again. Andrew got off the car to try and buy a road map at a service station but after a few steps he was stopped by a man who wanted to buy his jeans from him. Today, unlike the last time this happened on the Moscow Red Square, he had an extra pair ready in the car, and made some business by selling one of his jeans and a T-shirt for 85 rubles.

The man then approached the car where Ann, Cathy and I were waiting and told us in excellent English he was interested in buying more goods from us. We asked what exactly did he want to buy and he says he'd buy anything we were willing to sell: our frisbee, our football, shoes, sun-glasses, anything. Tongue-in-cheek, I asked him if he'd be interested in buying Ann and Cathy. He got very serious and replied that I would not be laughing like this if I lived here and knew how hard it was to buy any of the objects we had in the car. In the end we did not sell him anything, somehow we were not comfortable with this man.

When we reached the camping ground just outside Leningrad where we had booked our accommodation the receptionist had a bizarre proposal for us. He said we could be upgraded to a proper hotel but on one condition: we were not allowed to ask why. Well, it was an easy one. So we accepted, did not ask why, and next thing we knew we had two rooms in the *Karelin*, a fairly decent if simple hotel in the city.

In the evening we went to town. Again shut churches dotted our serendipitous itinerary, but we saw this was a much more pleasant city than Moscow. The churches must have been really magnificent in their time.

We parked Giallina by the Neva restaurant, near the bank of the city's river by the same name. As we walked toward the restaurant, one man came up to me and offered 20 rubles for a crocodile leather belt I was wearing, but I needed it to hold up my jeans and remain decent and therefore I regretfully declined. Besides, the belt was a gift from one of my uncles and I would not want to sell it anyway. Our luggage was at the hotel so I did not have a spare one to offer to him, silly me. He followed me for a while and upped his offer to 30 rubles. No deal.

Once at the restaurant door (we had not reserved a table in advance) we were told we could not eat there because the whole restaurant has been booked for a private party, even though it was high time for dinner and there was hardly a patron inside. But the belt-seeking man, who was still following us, perhaps pondering whether to increase his offer, explained to the restaurant receptionist: "They are Italians and need to have dinner". (I did not understand anything of what was going on, but Ann did.) The receptionist went inside to confer with his manager and after a minute or so he came out and said yes, we could eat there after all, they would set a table for us. A waiter came running and led us to a free table for four. We were left to wonder exactly why they would serve us food on the basis of our "Italian" nationality.

This was a typical example of Soviet economics: the state-owned restaurant had no incentive to serve four additional meals for the night, to serve any meals at all actually, since management was not profit-driven and managers or staff could never be fired. The purpose of these enterprises was not to make money, or to provide a service, but to keep people employed. Why in the end they decided to feed us would remain forever a mystery. They did not overcharge us, they did not want to buy anything from us, they did not try and sell us any black market stuff. But for some reason they decided to work and feed four "Italians".

As a result we ended the day consuming one of the most luxurious repasts of our trip. Of our lives really: starter, main and dessert all consisted of different interpretations of delicate sweet-and-salty black caviar from the Caspian sea! The accompanying Soviet champagne was not as memorable but it was not bad and served the celebratory function that the abundant caviar called for.

When we were almost done the belt man barged into the restaurant and further increased his offer to 50 rubles, I again said no and finally he gave up. I was almost tempted to sell him the belt after all, he was a nice guy and got us dinner, but it was a gift and the only one I had. We did pour him some Soviet champagne though, he deserved to be rewarded for his persistence and for getting us a great meal.

At this point a drunk Soviet sailor approached our table and asked if he could pay us to spirit Ann away. Andrew jokingly said: "Yes sure, go ahead". So I had to intervene and send the guy away as we were unlikely to get a good price! (Just kidding.)

Seriously speaking, I strongly regretted not having taken more stuff along to sell here. I knew one could sell trendy clothes like jeans on the black market but had no idea of the pervasiveness of local demand for so many items we just take for granted.

We were drunk with our good fortune and newly acquired bourgeois habits that we laughed all the way back to our hotel.

10 June 1980 – Sightseeing and dining in Leningrad

We woke up at around ten o'clock and drove off to town for some strolling and shopping along Nevsky Prospekt, the main high street in Leningrad. There was almost literally nothing to buy. Big shops employed lots of salespeople, too many for their size most of the time. Their shelves, however, were invariably empty, desolating scenes for the second most important city of the USSR and previous imperial capital. We had a look at the price tags of some staples, like meat, butter, bread. Everything was cheap, in theory, even for meager Soviet salaries, but nothing was there for anyone to buy.

Except for the *Beriozka* stores of course, where ordinary citizens could not even set their foot inside the door. Prices there ranged from uninviting to prohibitive, even for us. Maybe ok for some foreign diplomat or businessman, or some rich tourist, but not for four university students in a yellow Volkswagen Beetle!

We went for lunch to the *Sodko* restaurant where we had previously booked a table. Just before we walked through the door though, a couple of middle-aged men approached Andrew (for some reason black market dealers usually preferred him to me, I became a bit jealous) to ask if he had got "anything" to sell. He did not. We agreed we really should bring along more stuff to sell next time.

Not many choices were available on the menu but we did not complain: they had a fixed menu on offer for 22 rubles (about 25.000 Italian lire, or 30 US dollars at the official rate, about six times cheaper at the black market rate): excellent tender smoked salmon, spoonfuls of caviar which we could spread on excellent Russian buttered bread and Soviet champagne.

I can not believe I was actually even remotely contemplating such nonsense, but as we savored our delicacies I thought caviar was becoming a bit repetitive!

There was also a show of Russian folk music and dances, at the end of which a waiter came to our table, and only to our table, to ask us whether we had liked the performance. We had, really. He was happy and returned to the kitchen without asking the opinion of any other patron else. Who knows why? Maybe the manager wanted to make sure the foreign capitalists would walk away with a good impression and tell their friends back home.

We ended the day with a leisurely drive through the city. It was generally more pleasant than Moscow. We were lucky to be here during the "white nights": it was mid-June, the longest days of the year in the northern hemisphere, and at these latitudes the sun set very late, and briefly, so that even in the evening the sky was blue and it never got really pitch-black dark.

Leningrad was still mostly made up of grey Soviet apartment blocks, but here and there, amidst the grey concrete, the occasional pre-Soviet palace, or church, presented us with an interesting flashback into the former capital's imperial glory.

11 June 1980 – *Petrodvorets*: moose and rocket watch

We spent the morning at the *Petrodvorets* (Peter's palace, named after Peter the Great, the founder of the city), on the outskirts of the former imperial capital. The majestic palace of the Tsars, reasonably well maintained, rubbed sorely against everything the current regime has stood for the last sixty years, after the fall of the last emperor. But here it was, witness to history, and now used as a museum. There was a very long line to get in, but we were rewarded by the majestic halls inside, which resembled those of Versailles. Not by chance: Peter had commissioned this palace to keep up with the French emperor's.

It was very hot! Even too hot, incredible as it may sound as we were in northern Russia after all. So hot that it would have been nice to jump in a pool, but there was none. Actually there was one, but it was part of a monumental fountain dedicated to Samson at the center of the palace grounds. People were not allowed to take a dip, but a moose was swimming around and seemingly having a lot of fun! Yes, a moose! After repeated efforts, the museum's guards managed to pull it out of the water, but he jumped right back in. In the end they had to turn off the high fountain jets and lower some row boats into the pool to get the oversized pet out for good.

Andrew and I played some American football on the wide open lawn for a while. There was a larger than life statue of Lenin in a pensive, intellectual mood, sitting on a pedestal, and I sat next to him trying to imitate his pose and expression but without sarcasm, I did not want to get in trouble with some zealous party member that might be walking by. Lenin was the only Soviet leader to enjoy near-universal respect in 1980.

Some street vendor approached us trying to sell watches. I managed to buy a Soviet watch made in the local *Raketa* factory. *Raketa* in Russian means "rocket", and the logo suggested an association with Soviet space technology, which was quite advanced and justifiably a source of great pride for the nation. Pretty, sporty style, though the reputation of these watches was not as good as that of Soviet spacecraft. We would have to see how long it would last.

In the evening, we had booked tickets for the city's opera house, they would be performing Giuseppe Verdi's *La Traviata*, but when we got to the theater there was no opera. The program has been changed and we were offered a mediocre ballet performance accompanied by recorded music. Disappointing and unexpected as the city of the Kirov ballet company boasted a world-class reputation in the performing arts.

All was well in the end however, and we splurged for another caviar and champagne dinner at the *Moskva* restaurant. It was becoming almost routine, were it not for the our painful awareness that the supply of the little precious sturgeon roe would become much more expensive and essentially unaffordable once we returned to our side of the iron curtain. After our 52 ruble bill was presented, Ann (the only Russian speaker amongst us) overheard our waitress snicker ironically: "poor [as in moneyless] students!" Indeed.

12 June 1980 – Churches, gasoline, romantic white nights

Touring under the rain around Leningrad. At the Saints Peter and Paul cathedral all we could see was a few tombs of the Tsars. The cathedral itself, unsurprisingly, was not in use for religious ceremonies, but at least it was open to the public and not *na remont*.

Then we drove to Saint Isaac church, which again was open to the public but not used for religious purposes. We had to repress our laugh when we read on a poster that was hanging on the wall by the entrance that

> "in 1928 the people requested that the state take over the building from the Church in order to better preserve it and remedy the neglect that it had been abandoned to and because of which many artistic masterpieces were being ruined by time".

Right. Within it was an impressive array of colorful, malachite, jade and lapis lazuli, not to mention an impressive iconostasis before the altar.

Some older pictures of the building showed damage from WWII but at a closer look they were infantile photographic alterations to magnify the state's role in the restoration and its respect for religion. It was true that Stalin and the Orthodox Church did collaborate during WW II to defeat Germany, but that was but a brief exception and it did not last. On a wall there was a categorical and somewhat perplexing quote from Lenin: "The Church is an enemy of the people, not historically, but by definition". How can anything be something by definition but not historically? Never mind.

We climbed the stairway to the top of the dome which was ringed by a terrace, but once there we were informed by a sign in Russian that it was forbidden to take photos of the city landscape: military secret! Next to the sign there was a large bin with hundreds of film rolls, each film pulled out from its casing. We were warned that the rolls belonged to tourists who had violated the ban on photos. I had my camera with me, as always, but dutifully obliged and did not take any photos. I would have to remember the open views over the city and the river in my memory!

We then drove under the relentless rain to the Hermitage Museum, the second biggest in the world after the Louvre in Paris, which housed one of the richest and most famous collections of fine arts ever. Here it was allowed to photograph, which was a pleasant surprise. I supposed the Soviets were more interested in protecting "military secrets" than the intellectual property of their art. Many Italian exhibits, paintings and especially sculptures, the most amazing of which were no doubt those created by Antonio Canova, the neoclassical sculptor from Treviso. He did not work in Russia, but rich collectors from the city's nobility acquired the works of art between the end of the XVIII and the beginning of the XIX century, and then over time these masterpieces made their way to the state museum.

Miraculously, millions of items among the treasures of the Hermitage had been packed away and thus preserved during the horrific siege of Leningrad which lasted for 900 days of World War II. During the siege some 12,000 people found protection within the thick walls of the museum.

The best exhibit of the Soviet art department was a large low-relief map of the USSR which, we were informed by a sign in English, had "stunned viewers from everywhere" when it recently toured the world in a roving Soviet exhibition. Oh well, I was not really stunned but maybe it was just me. It was the museum itself which was actually quite stunning, for its exquisite late Baroque architecture and its grand layout.

We then drove on to buy some fuel. Unlike in Poland, here we had official and perfectly legal coupons and were prepared to pay the "foreign" price, but the lady at the service station did not want them. We guessed it was too much paperwork for her. So we paid the local price in rubles, only 6 rubles for 30 liters!! Basically free gasoline. The USSR produced millions of tons of oil every year, it was one of its top exports together with natural gas and guns, and fuel was heavily subsidized.

Evening dinner at the *Austeria* restaurant, where we again ate a lot of caviar while trying to spend all the rubles we had left, as tomorrow we would leave the country and could not take them with us. At the end of our meal the waitress proposed that we pay in dollars, exchange rate 1 to 1. Not so interesting for us. We counter-proposed to pay in rubles but gave her 8 dollars on the side for two bottles of *sovietskoe shampanskoe*. She accepted without hesitation and literally ran to the storage room to get the two bottles for us.

Back at the hotel we spent some time chatting in the terrace of our room, the pearlescent light of the white nights and the balmy breeze made for a very romantic setting.

13 June 1980 – Finnish border and ferry boat to Sweden

We woke up at 7am, gobbled up a quick breakfast and then sadly it was time to leave Leningrad. We drove slowly toward Finland, trying to take in the green landscape of conifers and beech trees. Brief stop at Viborg (Viipuri in Finnish), a town now in Russia that had been contested for centuries between Russia, Finland and Sweden. After a few steps around this town I felt I was "in Europe", in a was I did not when in Moscow or Leningrad. Everything went smoothly up to the check-point at the Soviet-Finnish border.

At the border we had to wait a good half hour before the Soviet guards even so much as looked at us. Then another half hour inside the border station itself. The first thing we had to do was change the few rubles we had left into dollars. The exportation of rubles was not allowed. Not that we wanted to take any out of the country anyway. The currency was not convertible and therefore could not be spent anywhere else. Still, we hid a few notes to keep as souvenirs.

We were slightly concerned about the two bottles of Soviet champagne we had bought last night for dollars, strictly speaking illegally, from our waiters friends. We were even more concerned with the Soviet Army belts we got from Igor in Moscow that Andrew and I were wearing as innocently as we could pretend, as that seemed to be the best way to be nonchalant about them. Luckily no one seemed to care about either our booze or our belts. This time the Soviet inspectors hardly even looked at our luggage. They completely ignored Giallina, I hope she was not offended by their lack of attention.

Once on the other side, the Finnish guards standing under their big white flag with a blue cross just waved us through their checkpoint. We reached Helsinki easily and quickly. What a relief, the roads were clean and smooth, service stations and convenience shops were lined with shelves stocking everything one can possibly need while traveling by car: food, drinks, real maps. We were back to normalcy.

At Helsinki Andrew and I needed to buy tickets for a ferry ride to Stockholm. Our plan was to visit my Swedish friends, the Ericson family. Ann and Cathy would spend some time in Helsinki with a friend and then head back to Poland. The *Silja* ferry line, the best one to Sweden, was fully booked. We got a place for us and the car on a *Viking* line boat. *Viking* was cheaper but the ferry did not really exist as a means of transportation between Finland and Sweden. It was a floating pub where kids from both countries could buy and consume cheap alcohol without restrictions.

Once on board, it was impossible not to notice that everyone, from 12 to 82 years-old, was completely drunk. We were not going to have a very social experience, rather an anthropological one: Scandinavians (and Finns: strictly speaking Finland is not part of Scandinavia, though it is quite close to it in many ways) trying to find any possible way to beat the system and get drunk on the cheap.

This crossing from Helsinki to Stockholm felt a bit like the beginning of the end of our trip to Poland and the socialist countries beyond the wall. From now on we would slowly work our way back across Europe all the way to Rome, though there was still lots of visits and fun ahead of us.

4. THE BEETLE GOES HOME

14 June 1980 – Swedish salmon and Soviet submarines

After a long night spent listening to the moans of drunken blond and blue-eyed people of all ages, we arrived in Stockholm at 9 o'clock in the morning. The plan was to visit the Ericsons, the parents of my high-school girlfriend Karin. I had lost touch with her, but her parents never forgot to write to me for my birthday, and we had kept in touch over the last few years.

I did not have their phone number with me. I had not been able to advise of our arrival, though I had told them months ago we could come by in the summer. They had always said I was welcome any time, and I knew they meant it. So we just drove to the Ericsons' apartment in Hasselby, in the outskirts of Stockholm. It was a green middle class neighborhood, lots of flowers all around. Quite a change from the last time I was here, a few years earlier, in the depth of winter, with sub-zero temperatures and all the flora either frozen stiff or covered in snow. However, there was no one at home. What to do?

We then drove to the coastal town of Oxelösund, where I knew they had their summer house. No one to be seen there either. Unusual. We waited a bit and had a light lunch. I remembered the Ericsons used to hide the key to the house behind a wooden pillar by their main door, and in fact it was there, but it did not feel right to just barge into the wooden cabin in their absence. I did plan to do so come night time however if they did not show up. I knew they would want me to. After a while however Bo and Ulla-Britt Ericson arrived. Ulla-Britt looked a bit surprised but kept smiling, Bo was enthusiastic as usual.

We were fed abundantly with various kinds of smoked fish from the Baltic, my favorite was always salmon. Then the four of us set out on the Ericsons' small outboard-powered wooden boat to go fishing in the archipelago.

These cobalt blue waters always brought to mind the USSR to me as a young student of defense affairs. It was here that the Swedish navy had repeatedly spotted unidentified submarines – widely assumed to be Soviet boats – trying to make their way around the shallow rocks and test the defenses of the nearby Swedish naval base at Karlskrona. The USSR had always denied its subs crossed into Swedish territorial waters, but who believed them?[31]

I kept looking at the quiet waters to see if a periscope emerged, it would have made quite a photograph. I also tried to pay attention to my hook and feel if a tender wild salmon would be kind enough to bite.

No luck today... we saw neither fish nor subs.

15 June 1980 – Car washing and net fishing

Relaxing morning at the Ericsons'. We needed to wash Giallina from all the black tar that stuck to its sides during our drive from Moscow to Novgorod, when we rolled at speed over a highway while it was being built! Rest of the day at rest. The previous weeks had been intense and we did not mind putting our feet up for a few hours. It was a sunny day in Sweden, warm enough to wear T-shirts, the beer was cold, and it felt just perfect.

We also spent some time in the family's sauna, just next to the water. It was in there that a few years earlier I had experienced the cultural shock of sharing the confined space on the wooden bench with my girlfriend, her parents, her sister, her sister's boyfriend and a neighbor or two who happened to show up, all in the nude. Coming from conservative Catholic Italy I was not used to be naked in anyone's presence, let alone young, blond and blue-eyed naked foreign females.

Long chats with the Ericsons, we had a few years to catch up on. They asked a lot of questions about the United States and Georgetown. I asked about Karin, who they said had got a good job, was living with a nice guy and came to visit once in a while. We also called Lena, her older sister, and planned to meet when we would drive to Stockholm to catch our ferry back to Poland.

---

31 *Just over a year later, in October 1981, a Soviet submarine ran aground relatively close to our fishing area, thus putting to rest any residual doubts anyone could still have about the issue. The Soviet navy claimed with a straight face that it was an isolated accident, that the sub just got lost, that it would never happen again. Right. After protracted negotiations the Swedes allowed the sub to be towed away and return home.*

In the evening we went out again with their small boat, this time trying to catch salmon with a net. It was illegal, strictly speaking, to fish with a net in these waters, but many normally law-abiding Swedes did it anyway for their own personal consumption. We did get some tasty fish to grill for dinner but, alas, no salmon.

16 June 1980 – Flags, friends and ferry

We left Oxelösund and the Ericsons after a breakfast heavily loaded with fishy proteins at 11 o'clock. In town I managed to buy a Swedish flag. For many years I had collected, and put up on walls around my apartment in Rome, flags from many of the countries I visited around the world. I always wanted a Swedish flag because of the special significance of this country in my life, but did not manage to do so until now. When I was dating Karin in 1977 I asked her about buying a flag and she recommended I write to the king. I was a bit taken aback by her unexpected suggestion but did not demur.

So I did write to the King of Sweden to the effect that I was going to get married with a Swedish lady and we wanted a flag from him as a kind of blessing. I did not really lie, we were a real couple (as sixteen-year-olds can be, and I did, genuinely if naively, consider spending the rest of my life with her) and in theory we could have been married at some point in the future. The secretary of the king wrote that he had no flags to give away; however, she sent me a black and white wedding picture of the king and the queen. I would have to wait another three years to buy my very own Swedish flag.

When the blue and yellow flag was properly folded in my suitcase, we drove to Stockholm and met Lena. She was as jovial and stunningly beautiful as three years earlier, although this time, sadly, we did not share time in the family's sauna. Instead, we had an ice cream while strolling in the pretty downtown area, and after saying good bye Andrew and I hit the road again, direction Nynäshamn, a small port town where we boarded a ferry headed for Gdansk. Back to Poland, again on the other side of the iron curtain.

When Churchill first coined the term, he said the "iron curtain" was running from Trieste to Stettin, just a few dozen kilometers to the West. It was 1946 and East Germany had not yet been completely incorporated into the Soviet satellite system, so it was not yet "on the other side" of the curtain. Once again we left the world of capitalist opulence to return to the penury of real Polish socialism.

And yet I had a clear feeling of coming home.

17 June 1980 – Ferry across the Baltic and back to Warsaw

Our ferry docked at Gdansk harbor in the early afternoon. It had been a quiet sailing, quite different from that of a few days ago from Finland to Sweden. Lots of Poles on the ship: Sweden was one of the few western countries that granted visa-free access to Polish tourists and they took advantage of it as much as they could. For tourism, for business, and especially for trading, at the edge of legality, all the goods they could buy in Sweden and that were out of reach in Poland. Sweden was surely capitalizing on its neutral role in the Cold War.

Smooth ride to Warsaw and evening in our dorm with Romek, Stefan and the rest of the SGPiS student crowd. We told our stories from the USSR over *kanapki* and vodka, and our Polish friends never lost a chance to sneer at the Russians. Stefan said he would gift all his Soviet paraphernalia (belt buckles, pins, medals, etc.) which he had bought over the years, or had received in his official capacity, to Andrew and me. We had shown interest in such objects as souvenirs, and he did not want to be near them any more. Since we first met him he had become progressively hostile to socialist officialdom and the USSR in particular. Something had shaken him but we would never know what. Or maybe he had given up on trying to improve the system from within, as an official, because he realized it was not improvable.

18 June 1980 – Crystals and corals

Easy day of rest at the dorm: laundry, catching up with our classmates, some *kanapki*, some vodka, small talk. Most colleagues were interested in our experiences in the USSR, though no one had much good to say about the country.

In the evening I went and met Marian and Ewa at their place. News of our shipment to Italy was not good: my crystal vase had been broken on its way. The big atlas and my old Tsarist rubles made it OK through customs and the rough handling of LOT Polish

Airlines though. There was no choice, Alitalia was not flying to Warsaw. Even Alitalia (not exactly the pride of my country) was usually better that flag carriers from Comecon countries. I longed for a time when flag carriers would not exist any more. Why should governments have anything to do with flying people and cargo around? They should of course regulate the air transport business, but not run it.

Marian and Ewa were very kind, they got me a new crystal vase! And one for Andrew! They also had a gift of corals for my mother and another set of corals he wanted to sell in Italy and which he kindly asked me to smuggle out of the country, which I agreed to do. I was not sure why corals were such a good deal in Poland. But they were.

19 June 1980 – Getting ready to leave, and next steps

In the morning we went to meet the Rector of our university. It was a formal meeting arranged at the end of our program, they told us he wanted to know how it all had been working out for us. We would happily convey our enthusiasm for the experience we had had. We were sorry it was coming to an end and somehow we wanted it to continue. We were not happy to stop here and just go back to our normal classes. And we wanted to make it possible for at least some of our Polish colleagues to come to our university.

Andrew and I had thought of a plan: we would organize a two-pronged student seminar meeting between Georgetown University and SGPiS, one event each in Washington, DC and Warsaw. It could do much to improve understanding and it surely would be lots of fun. The Rector agreed but, as expected, said he had little money at his disposal to contribute except for hospitality expenses in Warsaw. We would have to take care of the rest (all flights for the students, hospitality in the US) from the US side. We said we would try our best.

This highly intellectual endeavor was followed by a more mundane one: buying Russian caviar in the Praga neighborhood of Warsaw that was famous for a farmers' market. Or fishermen's market. Or Soviet traders' market. Here you could find Russians who had the right connections to buy caviar (or gold, diamonds, furs...) at subsidized prices in the USSR and then sold it at enormous profit in

Poland. Sometimes to Poles, in the best case to westerners who paid convertible cash. US dollars and Deutsche marks from West Germany were the preferred currencies, though British pounds, Swiss francs and even Italian lire were accepted, but the exchange rate they offered was not so favorable. King dollar reigned in Poland.

We bought half a kilo of premium Beluga caviar to eat ourselves over the next few days. I also bought a huge can of 2 kg which I planned to resell once we reached Italy, maybe to a restaurant or a luxury hotel. Or to eat it there with family and friends if I could not sell it.[32]

Romek presented me with a beautiful brown fur hat. I had seen him wearing it last winter and always loved it. I was not sure what animal it had belonged to and did not want to ask. I think it was rabbit. It was not the season to wear it now but it would come in handy in Washington next winter.[33]

One last currency exchange. I bought some Czechoslovak koruna from Marian. Kept some and sold some to Pat in exchange for some of his Hungarian forint. We would be driving through both countries and needed a bit of each. Our professionalism in foreign currency black market deals had reached enviable levels of sophistication.

In the evening we started packing our various crystals and caviar cans together with dirty clothes, paintings, towels and the rest of our belongings. It was a challenge to fit everything in Giallina's trunk. Also, while there where only three of us in the car on the way north from Italy last February, now we had Cathy, so that made it four. But somehow we did it. We even stuffed the back seat of the car with cans and boxes, all tightly wrapped in bath towels. We had reasonable hope they would not take the car apart at the various borders we were supposed to go through on the way south to Italy. East European customs officials were never expected to be as thorough as their Soviet colleagues.

If they stopped us at the Czechoslovak border, the first out of Poland, and asked about all the crystal, we planned to say we bought it with our student stipend. The rules said that we were entitled to

---

32 *In the end I did a bit of both: we ate about 1kg with friends and family and I sold the rest to a restaurant.*

33 *As it turned out, I would wear it for several decades and it was still in my closet over forty years later.*

spend up to half of it on domestic goods and export them duty-free. It was hardly believable we could have managed to live just on the other half of the stipend, but it was their law. We were confident that we were going to be safe.

20 June 1980 – Last day in Warsaw, for now

Andrew and I went to the girls' dorm after breakfast, but they were not there. They were supposed to return yesterday from their tour of Finland and northern Poland. We were slightly worried, not that anything serious was likely to have happened (though you never knew) but we had planned to start our trip back to Italy tomorrow. We had no urgent reason to return to Italy, we could stay a bit longer in Poland if needed though this would probably mean going through the bureaucratic process to get yet another visa, and we had no desire for that.

Then Marek, Marzena's brother, called our dorm to say everything was fine: Ann and Cathy were in Warsaw, they had arrived in Gdansk with the night ferry from Helsinki at 9 o'clock, and managed to hop on a plane on to Warsaw. They just had not had a chance to call us. We were relieved!

The afternoon was spent looking after our luggage and especially the last bits of paperwork. We needed to collect a Polish exit visa, a transit visa to get us through Czechoslovakia, where we did not plan to spend any night, just drive through, and an entry visa into Hungary, where we would try and find a place to sleep for a night or two. By 5:30 in the afternoon our passports were decorated with a new collection of colorful stamps and we could relax. The most difficult one to get was the Polish exit visa: after several months here we need to prove that our course was over, our stipend was properly accounted for, our onward visas were in order. A friendly lady at the visa office somehow liked us a lot and put our papers on top of the pile, just to be nice. She did not ask for money. She was generous with her smiles.

We then went to say good-bye to Marian and Ewa. I decided to buy a silver and marble clock they wanted to sell, to gift to my parents. It was very pretty and small enough not to create a great problem for our already very full car. Because there were no official receipts, I was, strictly speaking, not allowed to export it. Silver was one of those precious metals that, if you could find it on the black market, was very cheap here, so the authorities wanted to prevent its contraband.

Final dinner of genuine and hyper-nutritious home-made Polish food at Marzena's home. The kind that was often impossible to find in the shops but that her family could manage to squeeze out of the black market. Or "free market" as, more appropriately, it was called here.

She, always a melancholy type, wept a bit, her mother more. In fact we all did, though we guys tried to hide it.

21 June 1980 – Drive to Przemysl

We were ready to leave Warsaw at 9:30am. We took a few last pictures together with our Polish classmates and friends in front of our dorm at Madalinskiego. All of them came to say goodbye: Stefan, Romek, Marzena, Marek, Ella, Bonga, Elżbieta, Alina, Leszek, Tadek. Marta the engaged *kommunistka* did not show up, but then again she was probably busy with wedding preparations This was it, our last departure from Warsaw, not for a drive around the ever surprising country or for a journey through the mysterious USSR, but to go home.

It had been immensely interesting and fun to spend these four months in Poland. I knew I would be back, though I did not know when. Marzena would come visit me in Italy soon.

Just before leaving the capital, we filled Giallina's tank with our very last black market gasoline from good old Jan's gas station. Over the last few months he had become, if not quite a friend, as I could hardly communicate with him, and in any case we did not want to loiter longer than necessary when buying black market gasoline, surely a trusted point of reference of our Polish life.

The drive to Przemysl was smooth and easy. Funny I should think of it in these terms. A few months ago I would have described Polish roads in less positive terms, but I guess we had gotten used by now.

Once there, we meet Cathy's auntie, her father's sister. She had been waiting for us. She could only offer one room to the four of us in her small apartment, but it would do. We would squeeze in together as we had become used to do, this time Andrew and I in one bed and the girls in the other. There was no hot water and no sewage in the building, a strange smell whiffed out of the toilet, but we did not mind the small hardship.

This family was clearly not rich, not even middle-class, but very hospitable nonetheless. Dinner was based on *kanapki*. After which, three ladies and one man, all in their thirties, not sure who they were, friends of the auntie's we guessed, arrived and offered to take us for a tour of the town. Nothing much, but it gave us a good idea of a different Poland than that we had seen so far in Warsaw and other major cities. Poorer conditions, simpler ways, darker roads, a more basic urban setting that felt a bit like travel back in time. Same warm hospitality though!

22 June 1980 – Hungarian police and lake Balaton

We woke up at 8 o'clock after a good night's sleep and headed out to visit the house where Cathy's father lived before emigrating to the United States. It was a modest building but in fairly good shape. We wondered what it must have looked like when he grew up here.

For lunch Cathy's family served us some hearty *borszcz*, a soup with lots of proteins and vitamins to take us through the day. After which we bade farewell and headed south, toward the border with Czechoslovakia. No problem with Polish customs, all our stuff got through, no questions asked.

We were back in Czechoslovakia and this time we managed to get through the country without getting lost or running into Warsaw Pact military bases. Could not help but notice the innumerable monuments to Soviet military equipment that dotted the road, old tanks, relics of artillery pieces. Even an American C-47 *Dakota* aircraft, with the Soviet Air Force livery and a big red star on its tail: it had been given to Stalin by Roosevelt to fight the Germans. Some had huge billboards next to their platforms calling for world peace under socialism and denouncing the aggressive plans of imperialism. No one seemed to pay any attention to them. Kind of eerie, anyway better than the other, active, military we met when we transited northbound last February. We remembered that day vividly and could not wait to get out of the country.

We reached Budapest in the late afternoon and started looking for a hotel, but prices were way too high for our budget, so we decided to drive on. Too bad, as Budapest, together possibly with Prague, was the most charming of eastern European capitals.

As we progressed along the main highway we stopped occasionally to look for a place to sleep. Some camping grounds were cheap enough but fully booked. We decided to drive on toward Yugoslavia, maybe all the way to Italy!

At this point two policemen stopped us and started looking for trouble. They checked our passports, Giallina's papers, our tires, but everything was in tip top condition, which actually was pretty remarkable given what the little car had gone through over the last few months. Eventually they found that the light bulb of Giallina's rear number plate was dead. They said we had to pay a fine of 200 forints (about 10 official US dollars, there was almost no black market for currency here, the black rate was abut 30, "only" fifty percent higher). We could pay but their attitude was irritating and we decided to dispute the fine. What followed was an endless discussion, they were clearly trying to take advantage of us foreigners to pocket some cash for themselves. But we finally managed to tire them out so they let us go and we drove on.

It was pretty late when we reached lake Balaton and found a nice little hotel for 5 dollars per room! We were not sure exactly where we were, but the area was pleasant and well maintained. Balaton was the main resort region of Hungary and a destination for many tourists from the socialist brother countries. Our fleeting impression of Hungary was that the average standard of living was higher than in Poland.

My Soviet *Raketa* watch started to behave funny, it lost minutes per day, I could see it would not be much use for time-keeping purposes though it was still a cute symbolic souvenir of the USSR.

23 June 1980 – Through Yugoslavia and on to Italy

We left Lake Balaton at 10.00am. It would have been nice to spend more time here, after four intense months, and relax a bit, take in the cool atmosphere and sip Hungarian wine, by far the best that was coming from the brotherhood of European socialist countries. (Georgians might disagree.) In any case, their sparkling wine much better than the Crimean "champagne" we had drunk in the USSR.

The road was just OK and we proceeded slowly toward Yugoslavia. No problem with this border. Two socialist countries, Hungary and Yugoslavia, were, in theory, ideological siblings. In practice, Yugoslavia had long been pursuing its own version of socialism, quite open to contacts with the West and relatively more relaxed at home. It was a member of neither the Warsaw Pact nor Comecon. In general, the standard of living in Yugoslavia was higher than in other socialist countries, especially in the northern republics of Slovenia and Croatia. According to some statistics Slovenia's per capita income was higher than Austria's. Which is one reason why these two constituents republics of Yugoslavia were not so happy to subsidize their poorer southern cousins, the likes of Kosovo, Macedonia and Bosnia-Herzegovina.

It was therefore surprising that the roads we found in Yugoslavia were worse than in Hungary or Poland. Once we reached the border with Italy at Nova Gorica, the Yugoslav half of the Italian town of Gorizia, I pulled into a service station to fill up Giallina. Gasoline was much cheaper here that in Italy, so I wanted to make sure we topped up as close to the border as possible. As you got close you began to feel in Italy, the architecture was Italian and most people spoke the language. Even more people spoke Slovenian on the other side of the border. These lands had changed hands many times in history and the population was mixed.

The man at the pump spoke excellent Italian and said he only agreed to sell us fuel because he saw Giallina had a Roman plate.[34] He said he normally refused to sell to Italians from Trieste and Gorizia, who just crossed the border to take advantage of subsidized Yugoslav fuel. Border inhabitants of both Italy and Yugoslavia could go shopping in each other's country fairly easily, and while Yugoslavs went to Italy to buy consumer goods they could not find at home, Italians hopped beyond the border to buy cheap subsidized staples, fuel first of all.

We reached Mestre at about 9:00pm and got a couple of rooms at the *Garibaldi* hotel. Then out for a real Italian pizza. Nice to be back in Italy, I enjoyed hearing Italian and soaking in the warm air,

---

34 *In Italy at that time you could tell in which city a car was registered by the first two letters on the plate. Rome was easy as, uniquely, the whole name* "Roma" *was spelled out on top of the plate!*

though everything now seems soooo expensive! A pizza here was more expensive than a gourmet fine dining experience in Warsaw!

24 June 1980 – Back to the starting line

We spent the morning in Venice, just showing Cathy the highlights. Somehow I found some Soviet rubles in my pockets and managed to change them, at a very unfavorable rate, at a money changer in Piazza San Marco.

After lunch we got back into Giallina one last time for the home stretch to Rome. Mum, dad and my brother Fabio were waiting at our apartment, and a genuine Italian home-made dinner prepared by our family cook Anna concluded our trip.

It was over.

But I knew it was not really over. I knew I would return to Poland in the future, for personal and professional reasons. Marzena was scheduled to come and visit this Summer. Marian and Ewa surely would be in touch and we would try to make some money together trading goods between Italy and Poland. I was sure Stefan and Romek would be in touch and we would be able to continue our political conversations. Andrew, Ann and I had enough material for years of conversation and reminiscing. We would try and get funding for our student seminar in Washington, and hopefully fly some Polish colleagues over next year.

It had been the most instructive period of my life. I went to Poland because I was interested in the "real" socialism. Never a socialist myself, as a political scientist in the making I wanted to understand the thinking on the other side of the iron curtain, beyond the Berlin Wall. I thought better knowledge could foster mutual understanding among all European peoples, and peace.

The problem was, no one in Poland seemed to care about socialism. Some did not want to address the subject, or perhaps were reluctant or afraid to do so with foreigners. Those who did speak about it hardly ever said anything positive. It was different in the USSR, where some of those we met did seem to believe in their official ideology. What was clear to us, wherever we went, was that the system was not really working.

I would need time to sift through my memories and my notes, and make sense of all I had absorbed. For now though it was time to take in a good night sleep in my own bed!

SELECTED CHRONOLOGY

1939   August. Foreign Ministers Molotov (USSR) and Ribbentrop (Germany) sign non-aggression pact and secret protocol dividing up Poland and Baltic states into spheres of occupation and influence.

September. USSR and Germany invade Poland, carve it into two respective zones of occupation.

1940   Soviets kill over 20,000 unarmed Polish officers and intellectuals and bury them in mass graves at Katyn.

1941   Germany invades Soviet Union.

1942   Polish officer Jan Karski informs London and Washington about the mass extermination of Jews in Poland by the Germans but US and UK take no action.

1943   Germans crush uprising in Warsaw's Jewish ghetto.

Germans discover mass graves at Katyn, Red Cross places responsibility of massacres squarely on USSR despite Stalin's denial.

1944   Germans crush another Warsaw uprising by resistance movement, raze city to the ground. Soviet army halts operations on the other side of the Vistula.

1945   At Yalta, in Crimea, US, UK and USSR divide up Europe into spheres of influence, with Stalin implicitly handed control over Poland.

1949	NATO created in Washington. In the words of its first Secretary General, the British Lord Ismay, it was needed to "keep the Americans in Europe, the Russians out and the Germans down."
	Germany divided into two states: West Germany occupied by France, UK and US and East Germany by the Soviet Union.
	Berlin is also divided into two parts: a Soviet (eastern) sector as East Germany's capital and a American/British/French (western) sector as part of West Germany. However movement within Berlin remains free for everyone.
	Council of Mutual Economic Assistance (CMEA), dubbed Comecon, is created to foster economic ties among socialist countries.
1953	Repression of workers' demonstration in East Germany. Many walk to West Berlin and from there flee to West Germany.
1955	Warsaw Pact Treaty signed after West Germany is admitted to NATO. Communist Poland is a founding member.
1956	Hungary declares it is leaving Warsaw Pact. Soviet army invades and crushes rebellion.
1961	Berlin Wall is build in August, closing off only open emigration route for East Germans. Over 200 of them will die trying to jump over to the West in the next 28 years.
1968	Czechoslovakia tries "socialism with a human face" allowing limited freedoms but remaining as member of CMEA and Warsaw Pact. Armies from all

	European socialist countries led by the USSR, bar Romania, invade and crush movement.
1975	Defeated US leaves Vietnam. *Khmer Rouge* maoists take over Cambodia.
1976	Workers strike in Poland, demonstrations are repressed.
1979	Vietnam invades Cambodia, ousts pro-Chinese communist *Khmer Rouge* government and installs pro-USSR communist government.
	Short and inconclusive Sino-Vietnamese border war.
	December. USSR invades Afghanistan.
1980	Strikes in August challenge the Polish communist party's power. Trade union Solidarity is formed. Negotiations result in greater freedom and wage increases.
1981	December. Under pressure from Moscow, Polish communist party declares martial law and shuts down Solidarity.
1989	February. Last person is shot dead trying to climb the Berlin wall.
	June. First partially free elections in Poland.
	June. Hungary opens its border with Austria. Tens of thousands converge from all socialist countries and try to get through.
	November. Berlin Wall is opened for free passage and later taken down.

1990	East Germany is merged into a united Germany in the European Community and NATO.
1991	Warsaw Pact and CMEA (Comecon) are disbanded. Soviet Union ceases to exist.
1999	Poland, Czech Republic and Hungary become members of NATO.
2004	Poland and several other former socialist countries join European Union.

ALPHABETICAL INDEX

Afghanistan 2, 106, 113, 123, 145, 146, 148, 149

Austria 4, 6-9, 12-14, 22, 42, 56, 67, 110, 117, 127, 182

Beer 9, 83, 84, 95, 111, 133, 135, 173

Beethoven 41, 42, 44, 96, 195

Beriozka 157, 165

Berlin 61, 63, 69, 72, 77-82, 84-87, 131, 183

Black market 26, 29, 43, 54, 56, 58, 78, 81, 103, 104, 121, 131-135, 140, 143, 153, 162, 164-166, 177, 179, 181

Brezhnev 55, 62, 123, 155

Canaletto 27, 42, 47, 61, 104

Caviar. 54, 69, 70, 122, 140, 154, 162, 164, 166, 167, 169, 176, 177

Champagne 154, 155, 162-167, 170, 181

China .... 1, xii, 30, 35, 64, 65, 115, 123, 132, 139, 148, 149, 155

Chopin 44, 50, 61, 73, 96, 97, 100

Church 8, 34, 35, 43, 45, 57, 72-75, 79, 83, 88, 123, 134, 150, 151, 157, 158, 160-163, 166, 168, 174

Churchill 8, 174

Comecon 64, 98, 108, 109, 142, 156, 176, 182

Cuba 50, 51, 60, 61, 64, 107

Czechoslovakia. .2, 4, 9, 12, 13, 15-17, 27, 109-111, 118, 119, 145, 159, 160, 178, 180

Democracy..2, 9, 33, 36, 77, 79, 159

Ducks....................28, 29, 31, 46, 69, 96, 98, 123, 124, 129

Dzerzhinsky..15

East Germany...2, xiv, 18, 33, 37, 39, 51, 52, 61-63, 69, 70, 77-80, 91, 95, 116, 174, 183

EEC..98, 108, 109, 155

Elections..33, 45, 58, 112, 123

FIAT..12, 26, 36, 37, 123, 126, 161

France.........................8, 62, 80, 113, 116, 139, 156, 186

Gdansk.........................48, 82, 121, 129-134, 174, 175, 178

Georgetown. 1-3, 9, xi, xiii, 21, 22, 38-40, 60, 61, 89, 93, 101, 114, 122, 125, 173, 176, 195

Ghetto..50, 51, 111, 185

Gierek...42, 62, 104

GU..1, 3, xii, 15, 36

Hungary......................2, 27, 33, 67, 109, 110, 119, 178, 181, 182

Italy 2, 4-8, 10, 11, 14-16, 21, 23, 24, 36, 37, 48, 49, 53-55, 61, 66, 69, 71, 75, 81, 83, 88, 91, 92, 94, 96, 99-101, 104, 111-113, 116, 117, 121-123, 125-128, 130, 141, 142, 147, 154, 156, 158-161, 164, 165, 169, 173, 175-179, 181-183, 195

Kanapki..32, 46, 52, 67, 99, 175, 180

Karski, Jan..114

Katyn...67, 68, 92, 110

Krakow...............45, 67, 68, 101, 102, 110-112, 116, 119, 123, 141

Lenin....15, 56, 57, 62, 65, 100, 102, 146, 148, 151, 152, 155, 158, 162, 163, 165-170

Mongolia...64, 65

Museums.....49, 57, 80, 84, 100, 114-117, 131, 151, 156, 159, 161, 166-169

Music. 7, 9, xi, 41, 50, 53, 61, 72, 73, 75, 83, 88, 96, 129-132, 162, 166, 167

NATO...2, 8, 16, 19, 51, 119, 160, 195

Nazism........27, 49, 51, 68, 74, 77, 85, 110, 111, 113, 114, 155, 162

Olympics..112, 113, 146, 149, 155, 156

Pewex...24, 43, 157

PISM (Polish Institute of International Relations)...................54, 55

Police..15, 26, 30, 62, 66, 67, 77, 91, 101, 105, 124, 140-142, 145, 147, 154, 156, 158, 161, 180, 181

Pope.........................45, 57, 65, 66, 74-76, 89, 112, 123, 151

Red Cross...1, 68

Romania..110, 118, 187

Shopping.....25, 26, 71, 92, 103, 113, 115, 117, 124, 152, 156, 165, 182

Stalin.....8, 41, 50, 62, 63, 65, 67, 68, 110, 115, 118, 151, 152, 155, 162, 168

Sweden............xi, 170, 171, 173-175

UNESCO............38, 112, 115, 125

United States 1-3, 6, 8, 12, 16-18, 21, 25, 26, 39, 40, 50, 52-54, 57, 59, 61, 64, 65, 68, 69, 71, 72, 80, 81, 86, 88, 91-93, 99, 103, 107, 110, 113-115, 119, 121, 123, 125, 143, 148, 149, 153, 155-157, 159, 160, 165, 167, 173, 176, 177, 180, 181, 185-187, 195

USSR. 1, 2, 12, 27, 28, 35, 36, 41, 42, 48, 51-53, 55, 59, 62-65, 67, 68, 70-72, 78, 86, 89, 97, 106-108, 110, 118, 119, 122-124, 127, 142-145, 147, 148, 150-153, 155, 157-161, 165, 169, 172, 173, 175, 176, 179, 181, 183

Venice............5, 6, 27, 183

Vietnam............1, 64, 65, 69, 115, 149

Vodka.....22, 27, 32, 34, 46, 63, 67, 70, 78, 87, 89, 90, 95, 99, 109, 111, 121, 139, 161, 175

Warsaw Pact.....12, 15, 18, 109, 118, 123, 138, 145, 159, 182, 186, 188, 195

World War II....8, 9, 12, 49, 51, 67, 73, 77, 80, 82, 85, 87, 92, 109, 110, 116, 131, 144, 146, 151, 155, 162, 169

Yugoslavia............106, 107, 109, 142, 181, 182

ZNAK (catholic organization)............88, 89

ABOUT THE AUTHOR

Marco was born in Rome in 1959. He started traveling as a teenager with an Interrail trip to Scandinavia and never stopped.

He moved to the United States at eighteen and graduated cum laude in international relations at Georgetown University. During that time he also spent a semester in Poland and was arrested for accidentally trespassing into a Warsaw Pact military base.

He then earned a Ph.D. in strategic studies at M.I.T. in 1989, just when the end of the Cold War forced him to study everything all over again. He has lectured worldwide and published books and essays on international politics. He also contributed to the Italian Encyclopedia Treccani and ran research projects at the Istituto Affari Internazionali.

In Brussels he worked for many years at NATO, where he defended the Western way of life from all kinds of security threats and challenges.

He learned to take photos with manual cameras and Kodachrome film. Over time he became a SCUBA diver and a pilot of gliders and one fine day he decided to take his camera underwater. As he grew up he began to appreciate good wines – 1959 was a great vintage! He has fun in the kitchen and loves listening to Beethoven and cool jazz.

Later he went on to travel almost full time. He met his wife in the Maldives and they now live in London, where he has become a sommelier, writing about wines as well as travels.

His blog is www.marcocarnovale.com. Marco can be contacted by email at carno.polo@gmail.com. You can buy this book in paperback as well as kindle format on all Amazon markets.

Made in the USA
Monee, IL
14 October 2020